T0316558

# Native Advertising

*Native Advertising* examines the emerging practices and norms around native advertising in US and European news organizations. Over the past five years native advertising has rapidly become a significant revenue stream for both digital news "upstarts" and legacy newspapers and magazines.

This book helps scholars and students of journalism and advertising to understand the news industry's investment in native advertising, and consider the effects this investment might have on how news is produced, consumed, and understood. It is argued that although they have deep roots in earlier forms of advertising, native ads with a political or advocacy bent have the potential to shift the relationship between news outlets and audiences in new ways, particularly in an era when trust in the media has reached a historic low point. Beyond this, such advertisements have the potential to shift how media systems function in relation to state power, by changing the relationship between commercial and non-commercial speech.

Drawing on real-world examples of native ads and including an in-depth case study contributed by Ava Sirrah, *Native Advertising* provides an important assessment of the potential consequences of native advertising becoming an even more prominent fixture in the 21st-century news feed.

**Lisa Lynch** is Associate Professor and Director of the Program in Media and Communications, Drew University, USA.

**Ava Sirrah** is a doctoral candidate in Communications at Columbia University, USA. Previously, she worked on brand partnerships in T Brand Studio at *The New York Times*.

## Disruptions: Studies in Digital Journalism
Series editor: Bob Franklin

**Disruptions** refers to the radical changes provoked by the affordances of digital technologies that occur at a pace and on a scale that disrupts settled understandings and traditional ways of creating value, interacting and communicating both socially and professionally. The consequences for digital journalism involve far reaching changes to business models, professional practices, roles, ethics, products and even challenges to the accepted definitions and understandings of journalism. For Digital Journalism Studies, the field of academic inquiry which explores and examines digital journalism, disruption results in paradigmatic and tectonic shifts in scholarly concerns. It prompts reconsideration of research methods, theoretical analyses and responses (oppositional and consensual) to such changes, which have been described as being akin to 'a moment of mind blowing uncertainty'.

Routledge's new book series, *Disruptions: Studies in Digital Journalism*, seeks to capture, examine and analyse these moments of exciting and explosive professional and scholarly innovation which characterize developments in the day-to-day practice of journalism in an age of digital media, and which are articulated in the newly emerging academic discipline of Digital Journalism Studies.

**Mobile Disruptions in the Middle East**
Lessons from Qatar and the Arabian Gulf Region in mobile media content innovation
*John V. Pavlik, Everette E. Dennis, Rachel Davis Mersey and Justin Gengler*

**Native Advertising**
Advertorial Disruption in the 21st-Century News Feed
*Lisa Lynch*

For more information about this series, please visit: www.routledge.com/ Disruptions/book-series/DISRUPTDIGJOUR

# Native Advertising
## Advertorial Disruption in the 21st-Century News Feed

**Lisa Lynch**

Routledge
Taylor & Francis Group

LONDON AND NEW YORK

First published 2018 by Routledge

2 Park Square, Milton Park, Abingdon, Oxon OX14 4RN
605 Third Avenue, New York, NY 10017

*Routledge is an imprint of the Taylor & Francis Group, an informa business*

First issued in paperback 2021

*British Library Cataloguing-in-Publication Data*
A catalogue record for this book is available from the British Library

*Library of Congress Cataloging-in-Publication Data*
A catalog record has been requested for this book

ISBN: 978-1-138-04041-0 (hbk)
ISBN: 978-1-03-217869-1 (pbk)
DOI: 10.4324/9781315175119

Typeset in Times New Roman
by Apex CoVantage, LLC

To Zohar and Uma, who know what the fox says.

# Contents

# 1 Native advertising saves the newsroom?

## How news outlets came to embrace native advertising and how audiences and regulators grapple with its rise

A series in *The Atlantic* about the revival of Newark, New Jersey. Short web documentaries and long-form articles in *The Guardian* featuring stories from refugee camps around the world. A round-up piece on emerging threats, including cyber war, chemical and biological weapons, and drones, on the *Washington Post* website. A gripping multimedia package about fighting an Ebola outbreak in Sierra Leone in *Politico*. A collection of short pieces on Chinese business and civic life in *The Wall Street Journal*.[1]

These five articles – four from legacy media publications and one from a well-established digital news site (*Politico*) – are well-written, meticulously reported, and timely, and their subject matter is characteristic of public service journalism or international reporting. In terms of tone, prose style, and content, they mesh seamlessly with the other reporting to be found in their respective publications: still, they are . . . different. Each is set apart from "ordinary" editorial content by distinguishing fonts, layouts, or labeling: for example, the *Atlantic* piece uses a distinctive sans-serif font and has a banner across the top describing their series as a "Re:Think original," while the *Guardian* series is distinguished by the logo of "Guardian Labs." These labels identify these articles as native advertisements, content created by news organizations that is meant to appear almost, but not exactly, like the news you are reading. No matter how audiences consume news these days, ads like these are everywhere, and it is more likely than not that you have come across a number of them and not realized they were ads at all.

Native advertising is a growth industry, with global returns expected to reach close to 20 billion by 2018 (BI Intelligence 2015; Beer 2017).[2] Over the past five years it has quickly become the dominant or entire source of revenue for many of the digital "upstarts" in the news industry, and it is rapidly becoming a substantial portion of the revenue streams for legacy news organizations as well. In order to grow and sustain value from native advertising, news outlets are investing in in-house "brand studios" even as they shrink their editorial divisions; they are also partnering more aggressively with brands and candidates to craft advertisements that resemble, and compete with, their own editorial product. But though the consensus (for the moment, at least) is that over the next few years native advertising will become a more prominent fixture in the 21st century news feed, the consequences of this shift have only begun to be assessed by media scholars.

Building on the work of these scholars – as well as my own research into the history, growth, output, and future plans of media content studios – this book is an overview of the emerging practices and norms around native advertising, with a particular focus on advertisements which attempt to sway the reader's feelings about social or political issues. My argument here is that, though they have deep roots in earlier forms of advertising, native ads with a political or advocacy bent have the potential to shift the relationship between news outlets and audiences in new ways, particularly in an era when trust in the media has reached a historic low point. Beyond this, such advertisements have the potential to shift how media systems function in relation to state power, by changing the relationship between commercial and non-commercial speech.

This book is divided into five chapters. An introductory chapter provides an overview of the current debates about native advertising and current regulatory efforts around native content. In Chapter 2, I explore how legacy newspapers, legacy news magazines, and online news ventures are developing native advertising programs, describing how many are working directly with companies to develop, author, and distribute content. Chapter 3 looks more closely at a series of native advertisements focused on social issues and political campaigns and considers how these advertisements might speak to audiences and what ethical conflicts might arise as a result. In Chapter 4, Ava Sirrah a former employee of T Brand Studio at *The New York Times* – a content studio whose work I cite often in this book – provides a Case Study of the industry-side view of the native advertising process. Finally, in Chapter 5, I speculate about the future of native advertising, weighing the implications of either a news industry increasingly penetrated by native advertising or, alternatively, of an advertising industry that no longer relies on the news industry to distribute content.

The goal of this book is to help scholars and students of both journalism and advertising to understand the news industry's investment in native advertising, and consider the effects this investment might have on how news is produced, consumed, and understood. My principle critical lens is the field of journalism studies, but I use this lens as a means of making an intervention in a conversation that is as much about the form and shape that advertising might take in the future as it is about the future of journalism. In our digitally mediated future, the struggle to find a viable business model for the news industry is inextricable from a robust, pragmatic, and ethically-minded conversation about the effects of new kinds of advertising.

A note on the limitations of this study: I focus here mainly on the emergence of native advertising in North America and Europe, with the lion's share of my content examples and scholarly context coming from the US. Partly, this is because a good deal of the growth of native in the news industry has been driven by the global expansion of US online and legacy media outlets. As my survey of many of the major players in native advertising attests, US print and legacy outlets in the United States have been setting up content studios at a rapid clip since 2013, and their practices and examples have had a disproportionate influence on the industry.

This does not mean, of course, that there is not strong interest in, and expansion of, native advertising elsewhere. Arguably, the Canadian news publisher *The Globe and Mail* was the first "national" newspaper to embrace native advertising. The British-based *Guardian* and the BBC, among many others in the UK, both have large and ambitious content studios. And native studios are also emerging in Spain, Russia, Finland, Ireland, Norway, Latvia, India, and other places, with many shaped by regional media cultures and regulatory regimes. I document the emergence of some of these native studios in Chapter 2, but the complexity of some of those media cultures and regulatory regimes makes the task of a truly global study of native advertising too formidable for any single book. It is also important to state that just as the rise of native advertising is unevenly distributed, its effects are regionally variant in ways that extend beyond my discussion. Despite the forces of globalization, there remains a great deal of variation not only in the amount of news available in different places around the world, but also in the ways in which news functions in relation to the structuring of a democratic society (Aalberg and Curran 2012). What I describe here are potential challenges to a normative model of the media-democracy relationship, not to a given country or situation.

Like many journalism scholars, I was slow to develop an interest in advertising. Though I have always focused on the effect of new technologies on information delivery, I considered the study of the particulars of advertising, beyond the broader concerns of political economy, to be peripheral to the study of the civic function of news media. My feelings began to shift in early 2013, when the *Atlantic* magazine stirred up controversy by publishing a pro-Scientology "article" that was actually a poorly-labeled native advertisement. The piece, "David Miscavige Leads Scientology to Milestone Year" lauded Miscavige's work in opening new churches around the world and was timed to coincide with the release of a highly critical book on Scientology by investigative journalist Lawrence Wright (Voorhees 2013). The tone and content of the piece quickly alarmed *Atlantic* readers, who were doubly flummoxed when they attempted to comment on the article and found their comments would not post: Maria Einstein notes in *Black*

*Ops Marketing* that the comments were being moderated by the marketing team, who were deleting critical feedback (Einstein 2016). As Matt Carlson has documented in his accounting of the resulting fallout, publishers, advertisers, and media critics alike criticized the *Atlantic* for their initial attempt at creating a native ad: even the *Atlantic* quickly criticized itself, pulling the ad and issuing a public apology (Carlson 2015). But though some prominent critics of the Scientology ad insisted that the very idea of native advertising was an assault on news values (Wasserman 2013; Starkman 2013), others were more equivocal. Instead of criticizing the *Atlantic* for launching a native advertising campaign, they pointed to specific missteps, such as allowing the business side of the publication to moderate the article's comments section. Their attempt at constructive criticism – which Carlson describes as *norm-making* – was rooted in economic pragmatism. Even as the *Atlantic* set about assuring readers that it would reconsider how it handled native advertising campaigns, news publishers around the US and Europe were having discussions about whether their own declining revenues might be offset by starting a native advertising program.

Three years later, as I visited a series of US advertising agencies and news publishers in 2016 and 2017 and began to actively follow brand and content studios, I saw how quickly native advertising had taken over North American newsrooms and changed the conversation at advertising agencies. For agencies, the rise of in-house content studios at newspapers and magazines represented yet another lost source of revenue in an industry already in crisis; unsurprisingly, they were highly critical of what they saw as publishers' novice efforts to reinvent advertising. At news outlets, native advertising was discussed differently by employees on each side of the business/editorial divide. Those in charge of making the news outlet financially sustainable spoke enthusiastically about creating native campaigns that appealed to a publication's specific audience and matched the publication's tone and style. Those in charge of reporting and editing news on the editorial side, however, usually spoke of native advertising as something they knew was happening "over there," but not something to which they gave a great deal of thought or attention.

This twinned sense of opportunity and threat that characterizes the reception of native advertising in newsrooms reflects its status as a "disruptor" in the news industry, or a technologically driven shift in business practices that displaces conventional market relationships (Christensen 2015). As journalism scholars (e.g., Lewis 2012; Anderson, Bell, and Shirky 2012) have pointed out, the dire financial situation of the news industry has made it ripe for the ideology of disruptive innovation – prompting, for example, the Knight Foundation to embark on a program of funding innovative digital products that rethink how news is produced and delivered (Lewis 2012). However, as Lewis notes, such projects have rarely been aimed at preserving the institutional structures of the legacy press; instead they have sought to challenge or broaden what counts as news media, with the aim of radically changing the news industry in order to save journalism's core functions.[3] Arguably, native advertising does exactly the opposite – native campaigns are usually (though not always) sold to advertisers as a means to capitalize on a publication's history and prominence, providing advertisements for clients that channel the tone and style of a respected publication in return for a revenue stream that will hopefully help to sustain it. Native advertising is about *conservation* as much as it is about *revolution*, about keeping alive a news industry that has run out of other solutions.

So is native advertising disruptive? Yes. It changes the relationship between advertisers and publishers, helping to accelerate the permeability of the wall between advertising and editorial at news outlets. And over time, native advertising has the potential to substantially change the kinds of news that readers see and how they assess what they see, with potentially significant consequences for the democratic function of the press. Thus, although native advertising serves as a temporary (and partial) solution to the crisis in the news industry, it might also – paradoxically – disrupt the core functions of journalism in order to ensure the news industry's survival. As legendary *New York Times* media critic David Carr succinctly warned, "publishers looking to save the village commons of journalism through innovation should be careful they don't set it on fire in the process" (Carr 2013).

## Why native advertising?

If native advertising can be seen as the response to a series of crises besetting the news industry, then understanding native advertising begins by mapping the contours of these crises. As Rasmus Kleis Nielsen has noted (2016), the digital transition has engendered both *economic* and *strategic* crises in the news industry. Changes in the media ecosystem have decimated the market for print and digital display advertising, resulting in the downsizing or shuttering of news agencies worldwide and desperate attempts to find alternative revenue streams. These changes include, first, the shift from print to digital in legacy newsrooms; second, the rise of the "duopoly" of Facebook and Google and their capture of the digital advertising market; third, the emergence of programmatic advertising; fourth, the rise of brand self-promotion through social media and "influencer" culture; fifth, the rise of ad-blockers and other strategies of advertising avoidance; and sixth, the rise of mobile as a platform for news consumption.

## Moving online, losing revenue

The economic crisis brought about by the news outlets' online transition is a well-covered topic in journalism studies (e.g., Brock 2013; Siles and Bocz-kowski 2012; McChesney and Pickard 2011), so here I will summarize only briefly. Over the past two decades, as news consumption has shifted online, legacy news outlets have seen print advertising revenue decline quickly and sharply – in the US, for example, over 50 percent between 2003–2013 and 8 percent from 2014–2015 alone (Mitchell 2014). Over time, digital advertising revenue has grown, but the gains have not made up for print revenue losses; at the same time, many news outlets have been slow to establish paywalls and news audiences in many regions have become accustomed to reading the news for free. As media organizations have struggled to recoup their financial losses and develop online business models, they have shed staff while continually changing formats and workflows (Domingo and Paterson 2011; Anderson 2013; Usher 2014). In the US, the news workforce has declined by almost 60 percent since the late 1990s (Pew Research Center 2016); media outlets in other countries have seen a greater or lesser loss in workforce, but most have been affected.[4] Given these circumstances, some media scholars have become deeply pessimistic about the future of the industry, particularly in the US (Ryfe 2016). One report by the Tow Center declared "there is no such thing as a news industry anymore" (Anderson, Bell, and Shirky 2012, 1).[5]

## The rise of the duopoly

So where did the advertising revenue go? As news audiences would attest, advertisements in newspapers have actually multiplied as news has moved online; they have also become more obtrusive, with pop-ups and auto-playing ads continually hijacking the news reading experience. But the proliferation of advertising is a symptom of the problem. The price of advertising has plummeted online as other sites and platforms have emerged to compete with news sites for advertising dollars, many of which were quicker to determine how to track audiences and measure the success of ad campaigns (Greenslade 2016). Over time, as the media ecosystem has evolved, advertisers have largely shifted advertising spending to the two companies best at this task of tracking and measuring: namely, Google and Facebook. The catastrophic effects of Google and Facebook on media industry revenue became clear at the end of 2016, when analysts released data showing that the two companies had already absorbed half of the advertising market and were expected to earn 83 percent of each new ad dollar going forward (Kafka and Molla 2017). Looking at the numbers, Poynter columnist Rick Edmonds estimated that Facebook had diverted over $1 billion of advertising revenue from US newspapers in 2016 alone (Edmonds 2016).

The relationship between the news industry and the duopoly is highly complex, at once symbiotic and parasitic. For example, even as they compete with them for advertising, many news outlets – including *The New York Times* – are now dependent on both Facebook and Google for content distribution, as news consumers have become increasingly accustomed to getting their news from platforms and not individual news sites. This shift began in 2002 with the introduction of Google News, a free, global news aggregator that pulled headlines from thousands of news sites. While Google argued that their aggregator drove traffic to news sites, publishers saw a sharp decrease in home page traffic.[6] Over the past decade, as many news consumers have shifted away from aggregators and towards social media platforms, newspapers have struggled with using Facebook as a content distribution platform. Those who have opted for a strong Facebook presence eventually found it to be a Faustian pact: the use of Facebook increased their unique visitors dramatically, but also drove down the costs advertisers were willing to pay for each user, forcing them to stay on Facebook in order to remain financially stable (Madrigal 2017). Though both Facebook and Google have periodically launched efforts to help the news industry, news publishers argue that the duopoly has "failed to come to grips with the major collateral damage they have done" and the "media bloodbath" that has resulted. (Doctor 2017; Funke 2017)

*Programmatic advertising*

*The New York Times'* reliance on DoubleClick as a means of delivering advertising is an example of the ubiquity of programmatic advertising, or the use of advertising technology to algorithmically match advertisements with audiences. The automation of advertising sales over the past decade has made it easier and less expensive for advertisers to reach audiences, and ad-tech companies (including DoubleClick) currently process the sale of almost 70 percent of all digital ads (Urbanski 2016). But programmatic advertising is also often a "race to the bottom," with advertisers trying to negotiate for the cheapest possible advertising space; it has also trained advertisers to buy advertising targeted at an audience rather than tied to a particular publication, resulting in advertising that often appears out of sync with the editorial content surrounding it (Battelle 2014). Recently, programmatic advertising has also created reputational challenges for both news publishers and advertisers. Advertisers using some of the larger programmatic exchanges began to realize that these algorithms gave them little control over the websites that displayed their advertising or the content displayed alongside them, resulting in possibly damaging juxtapositions (Manjoo 2017). At the same time, news publishers have also become concerned that poor-quality advertising might distract readers or damage the reputation of their sites. There have been attempts within the industry to address this issue: in 2015, for example, a group of news producers including *The Guardian, Reuters, CNN* and others banded together to form their own programmatic network, and some programmatic ad agencies have formed "whitelists" that attempt to weed out more questionable publications. But many publishers and advertisers remain skeptical about whether programmatic advertising is the best solution for publications and brands careful about their reputations.

### *Brand communication*

As audiences began to spend more and more time on social platforms, advertisers such as Lexus, John Lewis, and JetBlue have also begun to complement display advertising with direct communication to their intended audiences via social media. Brand communication on social media platforms, like native advertising, is a relatively new advertising form with an evolving set of ethical and regulatory norms. But as any advertising agency will attest, it is has become an essential form of corporate promotion, and companies now divert money away from traditional advertising buys into social media campaigns that combine both "earned" publicity, such as viral campaigns, and "paid" publicity, such as mentions by celebrities and other paid influencers. As former *Forbes* writer and *Los Angeles Times editor* Lewis Dvorkin explains (2012), companies see this as a way of "brands disintermediating news professionals by writing and distributing thought leadership content," engaging directly with the public instead of through the filter of the press. This also means, however, that the press is sidelined in the process of communication, reducing both its share of advertising revenue and its perceived importance as conduit of communication to the public.

### *Ad blocking*

One of the reasons that direct brand communication has become so popular is that online display advertising, regardless of the platform, has become increasingly unpopular with younger consumers. Though concern about advertising clutter and the resulting tendency for media audience to disengage with advertising has been around since the 1970s, internet advertising has provoked a significant uptick in advertising avoidance (Rejón-Guardia and Martínez-López 2014), with digital ad clickthrough rates hovering around 0.05 percent (Chaffey 2017). Now, according to data from the Reuters Digital

News Report (Reuters Institute 2017), presently 24 percent of all desktop users and 7 percent of mobile users deploy ad blockers that allow users to access content without also seeing banner advertising. In response, some news outlets have retaliated by refusing access unless ad blocking is disabled (Cookson 2016), but the trend has nonetheless made banner advertising less attractive as a means of getting consumer attention.

### Mobile news consumption

One of the most recent shifts in news consumption has been to forgo desktop browsing entirely. News consumers have increasingly switched to using mobile internet and news apps as a way of consuming news – in some countries, mobile use has even outpaced desktop use (Reuters Institute 2017). Given the drastically reduced real estate on smartphones, publishers and advertisers have had to rethink the display ad, and native advertising has been promoted as good alternative. As Ponkivar (20154) explains, "Simply put, advertisers are quickly shifting their focus from traditional online advertisements, such as banner and pop-up, to native advertisements because sponsored or in-feed content plays better on mobile devices than display advertising" (1191).

## Native advertising to the rescue?

This brief summary of the news industry's formidable challenges should help explain why publishers have been searching for alternatives to digital display advertising. Due to the way it is targeted, sold, and formatted digital display advertising has become a broken revenue model, or, as the *New York Times* publisher said in 2017, a "nightmarish joke" (Morrissey 2017). To its proponents, native advertising promises a fix for much of what is broken: it is sold directly by media outlets to advertisers, allows brands to communicate in novel ways, evades ad blocking (Hajszan 2016), and displays well on the mobile web. Moreover, it is marketed as a premium product, and the prices commanded by good native campaigns suggest that advertising – whether print or digital – might once again be a viable source of revenue for news outlets.

But what exactly *is* native advertising? Ponkivar's equation of native advertising with "sponsored or in-feed content" aligns with the broad definition of the term embraced by the Internet Advertising Bureau, an international organization that coordinates the self-regulatory efforts of digital advertisers. The IAB describes native advertisements as "paid ads that are so cohesive with the page content, assimilated into the design, and consistent with the platform that the viewer simply feels that they belong." According to the IAB, this can include advertisements placed within the news feed, paid search results, and "promoted content" widgets serving content from programmatic servers.[7] In other words, as long as an ad is not a banner ad or popup, it is "native," even if it is unrelated content placed automatically on the page by recommendation engines like Taboola or Outbrain – and even if it contains little or no content at all, but merely "fits" the look and feel of a web page.

As Conill (2016) explains, the IAB's inclusion of programmatic content in the definition of native advertising stems from the origins of the term: the concept of native advertising has been developed not by news publishers themselves, but by the marketing and advertising agencies that they have begun to compete with. According to Conill:

> Native advertising is not a term with an established definition . . . most of its interpretations come from consultant and advertising agencies that aim to demarcate it as a monetizing strategy, a marketable product, or as revenue model for the publishing business. The agency Sharethrough defines native advertising as "a form of paid media where the ad experience follows the natural form and function of the user experience in which it is placed" (Sharethrough, n.d.). Outbrain, another online advertiser, defines native advertising in a native ad placed in the *Guardian* as a "sub-set of the catch-all content marketing, meaning the practice of using content to build trust and engagement with would-be customers"
> (Hallet n.d., in Conill 2016, 905)

These definitional variations reflect, in part, a larger definitional crisis in advertising itself. In recent years, rapid technological shifts have redefined relationships between advertisers, clients, and publishers so quickly that some have suggested that the idea of advertising itself needed to be rethought (Dahlen and Rosengren 2016). The slippery definitions also reflect the competing aims and turf claims of the various stakeholders in the industry: advertising agencies who want to retain a share of the native advertising business; publishing companies who increasingly act like advertising agencies; and advertisers who see continuity between content placed in editorial outlets and content placed on social media or proprietary sites. The end result has been confusion even within the industry itself, and repeated calls for clarified language.

However, though some parts of the advertising industry may benefit from blurry definitions around native advertising, content studios at news outlets largely market native advertising as an alternative to – and the antithesis of – programmatic content: rather than platform-agnostic advertising units created to serve multiple publications, native ads are created to seem like editorial output from one publication in particular, using that publication's tone and style to convince the audience that the sponsor's message is credible. Indeed, native advertising's recent success can be attributed, in part, to the reputational challenges faced in the programmatic advertising industry and advertiser's current wariness about placing ads in open networks (Gallagher 2017). Given this, it is not surprising that publishers and media scholars gravitate towards a narrower definition of the term, one that focuses more closely on the relationship between publisher and advertiser or the nature of the content.[8] For example, Sweetser (2016) states that: "native advertising describes a relationship between an advertiser and publisher wherein the advertiser (or third-party agency) borrows from the credibility of a publisher by paying to distribute content on the publisher's platform that resembles the publisher's own content in format and substance." Bell (2014) suggests that native advertising allows "brands a little closer to [a news outlet's] cool core." And Benton explains that:

> Native advertising . . . is seen as a place where publishers can still have something to offer. For Dell, attaching its name and content to The New York Times is something that's hard for a social network to match. For GE, sponsored content on sites like Quartz and The Economist attaches a vague innovation-friendly feeling to its brand. For the National Retail Federation, which has bought space for what sort of looks like an op-ed on Politico, native gives direct entrée to an audience of Hill staffers and political movers.
>
> (2014)

Still, if news outlets – for the most part – share a common desire to exclude programmatic advertising from their definition of native advertising, they are hardly united in how they label native advertisements, often coming up with their own typologies to distinguish between different forms of content that might be "branded," "sponsored," "promoted," "paid," or "underwritten." As I will discuss below, increasing regulation of native advertising has brought some order to the chaos of native advertising labels, but there is a resistance to developing industry-wide labeling practices (Deziel 2016).

A final definitional inconsistency clouds discussions of the size and scope of native advertising as a phenomenon: native advertisements are often given the label "advertorial," a term invented in the 1940s to denote advertisements that take the form of editorial content. This substitution appears both in news reporting and in advertising industry reports, albeit for quite different reasons. Those on the news industry usually use the term to express skepticism about native advertising; for example, a 2013 article in the *Guardian* scoffed that native advertising was merely "the politically correct term for advertorial" (Filloux 2013), and a Columbia Journalism Review piece labeled native ads "advertorials for the digital age" (Chittum 2014). But for those on the agency side of the spectrum, equating native advertising with advertorial emphasizes native's continuity with earlier forms of advertising and public relations, and suggest advertising's rightful ownership of the native advertising. Accordingly, a history of native advertising from *The Native Advertising Institute* notes that native advertising began "in 1915, [when] Cadillac ran an ad with the headline 'The Penalty of Leadership' in the *Saturday Evening Post*" (Laursen and Stone 2016).

There is no doubt "The Penalty of Leadership" is an iconic ad and a touchstone for the industry. A narrative ad crafted to resemble editorial content, it was created in response to rumors (allegedly promoted by Cadillac's competitors) that Cadillac had brought its new V8 model to market too early and that as a consequence the car was likely to be prone to problems. Instead of addressing the rumors – or even mentioning cars, let alone Cadillacs – "The Penalty of Leadership" described how artistic, intellectual and technical leaders paid the "price" of having to withstand the criticism of their detractors (Fox 1984). However, although Cadillac drew on the credibility of the *Saturday Evening Post* by placing the ad in the magazine, the *Post* itself had no role in creating the ad; instead, the *Post* treated the content as display advertising.

What I am describing here is different. Though advertising agencies would clearly prefer that they remain the content creators for advertisers, the rapid rise of content studios at news outlets is a distinct phenomenon, with its own set of ethical, logistical and civic consequences. The use of the term "advertorial" obfuscates these differences and makes it difficult to measure their effects.[9] So while recognizing continuity is important (and Chapter 3 will discuss advertorials at greater length), my focus here is on what happens when *news outlets* participate in the creation of advertisements that are meant to compete with their own news copy for the attention of readers.

## The native effect

The most frequently discussed effect of native advertising is its ability to affect readers in a measurably different manner than conventional print or digital advertising, with engagement rates at times approaching those of editorial content (Tadena 2014). A number of academic studies (Gillespie and Joireman 2016; Ponkivar 2015; Cameron 1994; Cole and Greer 2013; Kim, Pasadeos and Barban 2001) as well as industry reports (Lazauskas 2015, 2016; IPG Media Lab 2016; Elkin 2017) have demonstrated that media audiences pay more attention to native ads, remember them more clearly, and trust them more than conventional advertising. As Ponkivar notes,

> Native advertisements are viewed 53% more often than traditional banner ads. Not only do consumers view native advertisements more often than traditional ads, they also take subsequent action much more often after being exposed to native ads. Studies have shown that consumers share native advertisements with friends and family more frequently than banner ads.
>
> (2015, 27–28)

It is important to be attentive to what is being measured here – engagement – and what is *not* being measured, namely consumer purchasing behavior. The effects of native advertising on purchasing decisions remain unclear (Sahni and Nair 2016). But for the bespoke brand-studio advertising campaigns discussed in this book, direct purchasing is rarely the point; what is being sold to advertisers are campaigns that will entertain or concern the reader, with the secondary effect of improving brand image or addressing issues of concern to corporations. Evaluated along these expectations, native advertising is working.

Defenders of native advertising argue that it works because native ads are simply good content, embracing the rules of strong storytelling and providing a value to readers (Deziel 2016; Egan 2017; White 2016). But some scholars have argued this success is often dependent precisely on the degree to which native advertising is misperceived as *editorial* content. This criticism is not new to native advertising: earlier research looking at reader confusion around advertorials (Cameron and Haley 1992; Cameron, Jun-Pak and Kim 1996; Kirchner 1986) suggested that while the news format of advertorials provoked greater user engagement and recall, this was often because advertorials were confused with editorial content, even when labeled.

Recent studies of native ads have uncovered similar problems: in fact, the tendency of readers to consume media on platforms has made the problem much worse, as native ads can be seen by audiences that might be unaware of the labeling practices or customary format of the publication of origin. An industry study conducted in 2015 and 2016 by the media tech company Contently suggests that the majority of readers cannot tell the difference between native advertising and editorial – even if the advertising is labeled (Lazauskas 2015, 2016). Wojdynski and Evans (2016) caution their research on labeling in native advertising "suggests that the growth [of the industry] might not be because customers find it intrinsically compelling but because many of them do not recognize it well enough to develop the avoidance and defense strategies they have developed for other types of online ads" (166). Similarly, Aribarg and Schwartz warn that their eye-track studies of reader engagement with native ads "cannot speak directly to the long-term consequence of consumers being confused and feeling deceived as a result of mistaken clicks" (Aribarg and Schwartz 2017).

The potential deceptiveness of native advertising is the most common criticism of the practice and the focus of most native advertising regulation (as I discuss below). But media and legal scholars have suggested that a focus on deception misses some of the subtler or broader consequences. For example, several studies suggest that even when readers are not *deceived* by native advertising, they are *disarmed* by it. Taylor (2017) draws on Friestad and Wright's (1994) idea of "persuasion knowledge" to describe how media audiences approach advertisements with greater skepticism than editorial copy. According to Taylor, "The fundamental problem with native advertising is that, in the absence of a clear disclosure indicating that the message is an ad, the media outlet and advertiser are, in effect, blocking the reader's persuasion knowledge." In other words, readers have their defenses lowered when reading native advertising and are primed to accept persuasion rhetoric as information; conversely, when their persuasion knowledge is activated, they respond more skeptically or negatively (Wojdynski 2016). Combined with the credibility boost that native content gets from appearing on news platforms, this increase in credulity leads to an increased sense of trust in native advertising messages that is less the result of content than of the discursive environment.

In the advertising industry, perhaps unsurprisingly, the idea that readers' defenses are lowered when they approach native advertising is cast in a more positive light. At a conference on native advertising convened by the American Press Institute, an advertising executive at Oglivy explained that native advertising places consumers in an "interaction/conversation mode" rather than a "direct response buying mode"; this means they are more receptive to what native ads have to say (Sonderman and Tran 2013). At a panel on native advertising and the law at Cardozo Law School, advertising industry lawyer Rich Kurnit explained the difference in starker terms: audiences have learned to tune out ads, so brand messages labeled as ads might as well be marked with a "skull and crossbones": the best way for advertising to work is for ads to not resemble ads at all "Let's be clear, the word 'ad,' the word 'advertisement' is a complete negative," Kurnit argued, "this is why . . . my clients have done everything in their power to try to not use that word" (Kurnit, quoted in Goodman et al. 2016, 598).

On one hand, Kurnit's position – in effect, that native advertising should be allowed to be nearly indistinguishable from editorial content – is an extreme one. On the other hand, it can be seen as the logical outcome of the collapse of the distinctions between the business and editorial divisions at news outlets that remained a global norm from the mid-19th to late 20th century. As news organizations commercialized and professionalized in the US and then elsewhere, the often professed "wall" between business and editorial served as a means for providers to differentiate their content from market-driven information and thus claim special protections for journalistic practices and journalistic output (Schudson 1978).[10] But towards the last part of the twentieth century, as the digital transition created economic hardship in the media industry, the normative arguments for the need for a business/editorial divide slowly gave way to arguments that news organizations needed to integrate business and editorial divisions further in order to survive (Eckman and Lindlof 2003; DeLorme and Fedler 2005; Basen 2012; McChesney 2011). Among other changes, newsrooms embraced the use of commercial metrics to drive story creation, displacing customary editorial filters such as civic value or newsworthiness (Hindman 2017). By the time legacy news outlets began considering setting up content studios, the "wall" between business and editorial had, at many legacy outlets, become a porous "curtain" (Coddington 2015). At many digital news startups the wall was never erected, in part because native advertising was seen, from the outset, as a key part of the publication's revenue strategy.

Studies of attitudes towards native advertising in the news industry reveal that many in the industry itself fear native advertising is accelerating the collapse of the business/editorial divide and creating new ethical and professional minefields. The Native Advertising Institute found that almost 40 percent of publishers (including both news and feature publications) were concerned about the "lack of separation of the editorial and commercial sides of their business" when it came to native advertising (Laursen 2016). A similar survey of both publishers and marketing executives (Shauster et al. 2016) showed that both sides were concerned about a number of issues connected to the increasing penetration of advertising into the editorial processes of new outlets, including the perception that advertisers might be able to directly influence content, the potential for damage to both publisher and advertiser credibility, and the potential for damage to media's role in the democratic process. Even some of the strongest proponents of native advertising have cautioned against a too-close relationship between advertising and editorial (Hansen 2017).

Concern about advertiser influence is longstanding, with studies in the US and Europe showing that advertisers have long attempted to block stories, promote positive coverage, or push a given policy issue in exchange for advertising revenue (Soley and Craig 1992; Benson 2001; De Smet and Vanormelingen 2011; An and Bergen 2007; Porlezza 2017). But the growth of brand studios has raised the stakes by placing native advertising divisions in the chain of command at media organizations (Baker 2016). News publications including *BuzzFeed* (Stack 2015) and *Vice* (Allen 2014) have been accused of pulling content that might offend advertisers purchasing native campaigns. As the *Washington Post* expands its native division, it has recently established a social media policy that forbids reporters from making critical comments about advertisers on social media (Beaujon 2017).

Like the question of advertiser influence, press credibility issues predate native advertising (Brants 2013; Ladd 2011; Bakir and Barlow 2007). Still, the spread of native advertising has provoked fresh concern about maintaining trust in the media at a moment when credibility is quite low in many regions, particularly in the US.[11] Former *New York Times* public editor Margaret Sullivan warned that native advertising had the potential to affect credibility at the *Times*, writing that "these arrangements can bring inherent conflicts – or at least the appearance of them, which is almost as bad when credibility is at stake " (Sullivan 2015). Her concerns have been supported by a recent a study of news audiences (Amazeen and Muddiman 2016) which found that both legacy and online news outlets were evaluated less favorably for having native ads.[12] In a legal article assessing the consequences of increased native advertising, Lili Levi argues the reputational harm done by native advertising will lead to "news organizations with crippled reputations in their core functions, and unable to tap the commercial well for funding" (Levi 2015, 651).

Levi is one of several scholars in the US and elsewhere who have argued that the erosion of press credibility as a result of native advertising will harm the already-challenged ability of the press to play an active role in democracy (Liebes and Ribak 1991). Like Levi, Schauster, Ferrucci and Neill (2016); and Bakshi (2015) suggest that news outlets who are not seen as trustworthy because they run native advertising cannot engage in the accountability journalism central to maintaining strong democratic institutions. Kreiss (2016) has argued more broadly that the economic pressure of digital monetization has interfered with journalists' pursuit of the "civic skepticism" characteristic of an independent press. Such concerns resonate even in countries where the press is seen as more trustworthy; in *Blurring The Lines: Market Driven and Democracy Driven Freedom of Expression*, Finnish media scholars Maria Edström, Andrew Kenyon, and Eva-Maria Svensson ask how the press is to be trusted when there is no longer a distinction between "market driven" and "democracy driven" forms of content (Edström, Kenyon and Svensson 2016).

Aside from academic research, the depiction of native advertising in US popular culture also reflects a concern that native advertising has the potential to deceive the public and eventually erode press credibility. In 2014, HBO comedian John Oliver inveighed against native advertising in a clip from his show Last Week Tonight which has been viewed more than eight million times. Criticizing *BuzzFeed*, *Time Magazine*, and the *New York Times* for their native ad programs, Oliver quipped that "native advertising in news outlets is like combining guacamole and Twizzlers. They're both good in their own way, but if you mix them together, somehow you make both of them really gross" (Wemple 2014). In 2015, the Comedy Central show *South Park* aired a segment on native advertising as well, imagining a world controlled by native advertising, in which only two people retain the "superhuman" ability to tell native ads apart from news stories and some native advertisements have "evolved" into human form (Lynch 2015). Both of these television moments – though clearly satirical – suggest that the emergence of native advertising has been met with a fair amount of cultural anxiety. *South Park*, in particular, suggests that native advertising has turned into a bogeyman that is beyond human control, leaving news readers unable to tell the difference between information and persuasion (Shinkevich 2016).

## Regulating native advertising

The *South Park* episode provokes an obvious question: who is actually responsible for "controlling" native advertising? The answer is complicated, as each country has a different constellation of national, sub-national, and international regulatory regimes. To complicate things further, native advertising is also self-regulated, with varying levels of formality, by the oversight bodies governing the professions of journalism and advertising. Two overarching themes govern regulatory discussions on native advertising in both the US and Europe: how to determine whether and when such advertising is misleading, and how to determine when governmental regulation of advertising results in the restriction in freedom of expression. The latter determination has been hampered by what has been described by US and European scholars as an outdated understanding of commercial speech as it pertains to the idea of native advertising. If native advertising becomes as pervasive as its proponents expect, it is likely that a series of court challenges will further shift how commercial expression is regulated on both sides of the Atlantic.

### *The United States*

In the United States, native advertising is regulated by the Federal Trade Commission (print), the Federal Communication Commission (broadcast), and by various self-regulatory bodies including the Interactive Advertising Bureau (IAB). Additionally, individual states have developed their own laws around advertising, allowing consumers recourse to the courts when they feel they have been duped. The roots of advertising regulation date back to the Newspaper Publicity Act of 1912, which set requirements for labeling advertising and put an end to the 19th-century practice of "reading notices," or advertisements disguised to look like editorial copy. Advertisers paid for these "reading notices," precursors to both advertorials and native advertising, in order both to hawk products and influence public debate; by the 1870s, their widespread use prompted a public debate concerning truth in advertising. The newspaper industry resisted the regulation of reading notices, challenging the Newspaper Publicity Act in a case that reached the Supreme Court. The Court ruled against the industry, saying that the Publicity Act was a permissible regulation of the media in return for the reduced postal rates granted by the government (Blanchard 1992).

The Publicity Act brought an end to reading notices, but deceptive advertising practices remained a persistent concern in the US, with "waves" of regulatory reform and enforcement throughout the 20th century (Calfee and Ringold 1988). The most recent phase of regulatory reform began in 2013, after *The Atlantic* magazine's Scientology ad fiasco created concern about the potential for deception in native advertising. After holding a workshop in which regulators and industry representatives debated the need for specific rules for native advertising (FTC 2013), the agency issued guidelines and an enforcement statement at the end of 2015. Though much of the guidelines reflected existing practice, the FTC asked for two significant modifications: labels that identify content as advertising *before* the consumer begins reading the ad, and language that was completely transparent. To this end, the FTC gave a list of acceptable terms:

> Terms likely to be understood include "Ad," "Advertisement," "Paid Advertisement," "Sponsored Advertising Content," or some variation thereof. Advertisers should not use terms such as "Promoted" or "Promoted Stories," which in this context are at best ambiguous and potentially could mislead consumers that advertising content is endorsed by a publisher site. Furthermore, depending on the context, consumers reasonably may interpret other terms, such as "Presented by [X]," "Brought to You by [X]," "Promoted by [X]," or "Sponsored by [X]" to mean that a sponsoring advertiser funded or "underwrote" but did not create or influence the content.
>
> (FTC 2015b)[13]

The FTC's intervention was anticipated; still, many in the industry greeted these specific suggestions with dismay. One analyst described them as a "bombshell" (Critchlow 2016) and a publisher complained the labeling restrictions would limit creativity (Ember 2015). The IAB argued the guidelines were "overly prescriptive" (IAB 2015), characterizing the memorandum as an unwelcome solution to a problem that could be solved through self-regulation. In fact, the IAB had attempted to demonstrate to the FTC that self-regulation was sufficient by pre-emptively issuing their own set of guidelines for native advertising, *The Native Advertising Playbook* (IAB 2013).

Though widely used in the industry, the *Playbook* could be seen as part of the problem the FTC was addressing: though it calls for clarity in labeling, it also avoids the kind of language recommendations eventually embraced by the FTC, suggesting that labeling could take many different forms. And the vagueness of IAB's recommendations are in line with the guidelines of other US industry oversight groups. In 2016, when the National Advertising Division of the Better Business Bureau added native advertising to its Code of Advertising, they included a different definition of "sponsored content" than the FTC, suggesting that brands can be involved in its creation (BBB 2016). When the American Society of Magazine Editors published a set of native advertising guidelines in 2015, they suggested that print publications should use the term "advertisement" while online publications should use "sponsored content" (Mullin 2015). The Online News Association, the only press association to issue guidelines specifically for news publishers, has suggested that outlets use focus groups to find out which labels work best for their individual audiences (Kent 2017).

This inconsistency explains why a study of ads conducted in the wake of the FTC memorandum demonstrated a significant gap between the guidelines and common practice. "Promoted" remains the most popular label for native advertising, with "sponsored" coming in second; the label "ad" has only appeared 5 percent of the time (Swant 2016). This suggests that self-regulation may not suffice to rein in the worst tendencies of native advertising. Some legal scholars (Ponkivar 2015; Levi 2015) argue that self-regulation should be sufficient, but others (Bakshi 2015; Einstein 2015; Casale 2015) believe FTC oversight is needed given the persistence of deceptive labeling practices. Even Levi's plan for self-regulation would require a change from current practice, as he insists primary oversight of native advertising should come from the press, and not (as is currently the case) from the advertising industry.

Even pro-regulation scholars acknowledge that the greatest challenge to government regulation of native advertising: namely, that native advertising which does not discuss a particular product or brand (e.g., many of the examples discussed in this book) tests the boundaries between non-commercial speech, which is protected under the First Amendment, and commercial speech, which is held to a higher standard of verifiability. Since

1976, US courts have maintained that commercial speech has a degree of First Amendment protection if it is "hybrid" speech, i.e., speech that does not merely advertise a brand or service (*New York Times vs Sullivan* 1976).[14] Over the past few decades, numerous court cases have attempted to parse the distinction between pure commercial speech and hybrid speech, with mixed results (Krzeminska-Vamvaka 2008). One of the most relevant cases, *Nike, Inc. v. Kasky*, hinged on Nike's insistence that publicly defending its labor practices did not amount to commercial speech, and thus was not subject to verifiability. The case was heard and then dismissed by the US Supreme Court, a ruling which some saw as evidence for the judicial system's reluctance to make a final determination on the limits of commercial speech (Goldstein 2002). Given this reluctance, some critics have argued that the FTC is overreaching by setting out guidelines for native advertising that applied equally to all native ads whether or not they directly promote products or brands: in effect, they have expanded the category of commercial speech, by including native ads which some industry advocates believe should be classified as noncommercial or hybrid (Goodman et al. 2015; Bakshi 2015). As the FTC ramps up enforcement of native advertising, the industry may attempt to push back on the labeling requirements for such hybrid content.

### Regulating native advertising in Europe

Just as in the United States, native advertising in Europe is subject to both regulatory oversight and self-regulatory oversight. In Europe, however, the situation is complicated because native advertising is governed first, by The European Convention on Human Rights, which protects information freedom; second, by EU directives, which establish a baseline for truth in advertising; and third, by laws in individual European countries that can extend – though not limit – these regulations. Self-regulatory bodies in the EU also include both pan-European and national organizations; for example, The European Advertising Standards Alliance coordinates national advertising self-regulatory organisations across Europe, while the UK Advertising Standards Authority is a self-regulatory agency with control over Britain. The IAB also has both national branches and a European branch, many of which have issued native advertising guidelines.

EU advertising directives have generally tried to take into account existing national laws on advertising as well as US law, in order to create regulation that recognizes the cross-border nature of trade and advertising (Petty 1997). As in the US, regulation focuses on the question of misleading advertising. The primary directive relevant to native advertising is the Unfair Commercial Practices Directive (2005/29/EC), which specifically prohibits the use of "editorial content in the media to promote a product where a trader has paid for the promotion without making that clear in the content or by images or sounds clearly identifiable by the consumer (advertorial)" (Annex I, item 11) and "falsely claiming or creating the impression that the trader is not acting for purposes related to his trade, business, craft or profession or falsely representing oneself as a consumer" (Annex I, item 22). As well, the Directive on Electronic Communication (2000/31/EC), requires clear disclosure of "the natural or legal person on whose behalf the commercial communication is made."

In practice, these EU directives have met with several challenges. In 2006, the EU made a further effort to harmonize laws around misleading advertising, noting in the Directive Against Misleading And Comparative Advertising (2006/114/EC) that "the laws against misleading advertising in force in the Member States differ widely," and that such differences "hinder the execution of advertising campaigns beyond national boundaries and thus affect the free circulation of goods and provision of services." In 2012, the EU reported continued issues with defining what constitutes misleading advertising, as well as problems with consistent enforcement across member states (PLC EU 2012).

Given the complexity of European law, there is no clear way of addressing these issues. As Petty (1997) has noted, the EU countries have different legal standards for interpreting whether or not an advertisement is misleading; some countries allow a judge to make the determination, while others require consumer testing. And enforcement at the national level is complicated by the different regulatory histories of each country. In the UK, Belgium, Ireland, Italy, and Switzerland, self-regulation is the primary means of adjudicating advertising complaints. In Scandinavia, robust self-regulation exists, but countries also adjudicate advertising complaints through a consumer ombudsman position that is effectively a hybrid between a self-regulatory enforcer and the FTC. In German and Austria, most advertising regulation emerges as a result of private lawsuits. And France, Luxembourg and Belgium embrace a hybrid approach, with a mix of regulation, self-regulation, and regulation via lawsuit (Petty 1997; Greenslade 2012). As can be seen from the US example, self-regulatory bodies and regulatory bodies often balance industry and public interest differently given their different goals.

Finally, regulating native advertising in the EU is complicated – just as in the US – by the difficulty of determining what kind of speech protections native advertising might be allowed under law. Though efforts have been made to harmonize approaches (Petty 1997), the EU has a somewhat different understanding of commercial speech, one based on a notion of freedom of expression more equally grounded in rights and responsibilities.

Free speech protection stems from Article 10 the European Convention on Human Rights, which protects the "freedom to hold opinions and to receive and impart information and ideas without interference by public authorities." This notion of information freedom has been used to posit protections for commercial speech; in practice, however, cases in which the Court has held that the protection of information in the ECHR also applies to commercial speech have involved advertisements that clearly had a dimension other than commercial. The European Court of Justice, the court more centrally concerned with protection of economic freedoms, has generally seen cases regarding commercial speech through the lens of consumer protection, without establishing a distinct right of commercial expression. And both courts often cede to national laws when it comes to the regulation of commercial speech (Krzeminska-Vamvaka 2008).

In sum, the regulation of native advertising in Europe is even less straightforward than it is in the US, given the multiplicity of regulatory regimes, the need to harmonize between differing national traditions, and an even greater lack of clarity around the protections afforded commercial speech. Perhaps due to this complexity – or, alternately, due to the relative newness of native advertising in Europe, or to the fact that European publications may tread more carefully than in the US – there have been few cases where native advertising has attracted regulatory scrutiny.[15]

## Conclusion

This chapter has offered a broad overview of the emergence of native advertising, the central debates about its consumer and civic effects, and of efforts to regulate native advertising in the US and Europe. What should emerge most clearly from this discussion is that native advertising has been evolving so quickly that defining, measuring, and regulating native advertising is a fundamentally different kind of undertaking than the defining, measuring, and regulating of conventional display advertising. Native advertising has a number of competing genealogies and manifestations, leading to disagreement about what native is and how to measure its growth as an industry. It has different goals than conventional display advertising, with advertisers seeking more nebulous goals including engagement and brand positivity through association. Its existence in a murky area between advertising and journalism has led to a lack of consensus about the best regulatory and self-regulatory measures to ensure its integrity; beyond this, its influence on journalism as a profession and institution is still little understood.

At the same time, however, it is important to remember that native advertising is part of an ongoing effort within the media industry *to ensure the survival of that industry* in the face of the challenges also described above.

The next chapter examines the rapid rise of content studios at media outlets in the US, Europe, and elsewhere, noting along the way the challenges that have led these outlets to explore native advertising as a potential lifeline.

## Notes

1 In this case, the clients included Prudential Insurance, the UNHCR, the research firm Battelle, The Bill and Melinda Gates Foundation, and the Chinese Government.
2 This figure varies depending on who is doing the measuring and the calculating, given that there are different ways of categorizing native advertising (as I discuss).
3 As the historian Jill Lepore (2014) has noted, legacy outlets like the *New York Times* have described themselves as the victim of disruption: in its 2014 Innovation Report to justify its own efforts to soften the wall between advertising and editorial, the Times argued "a pack of news startups are hoping to 'disrupt' our industry by attacking the strongest incumbent – The New York Times," and that the Times needed to become more flexible in order to survive.
4 It should be noted that there are still countries – for example, India and Japan – where print media still thrives and the news industry is still relatively profitable.
5 As Pablo Boczkowski has noted, most of the empirical research on the decline in the news industry has been conducted on the US (Boczkowski 2004).
6 Google News has been challenged by various media outlets and governments in Europe and the US, and was shut down permanently in Spain in 2014 after the Spanish news publisher's association lobbied for a law requiring aggregators to pay them.
7 In fact, the IAB's definition helped to prompt programmatic advertisers firms such as Taboola to think of themselves as native advertising companies (Goodman et al. 2016).
8 There are a few broader examples: a 2017 whitepaper by the Native Advertising Institute featured a campaign about Norwegian film that was not produced in partnership with a media outlet; though the content marketer VG Partnerstudio hired journalists to work on the project, it was produced as a stand-alone website (NAI 2017).
9 It also creates regulatory confusion; the EU, for example, includes advertorials on their "blacklist" of banned commercial practices, even though native advertising is growing practice in Europe.
10 As Conill himself noted, it was a norm that often masked a more complex reality (Conill 2016).
11 According to the 2017 Reuters News Report, only 38 percent of US citizens had confidence in the US media, compared to 43 percent in the UK, 50 percent in Germany and Spain, and 62 percent in Finland.
12 Research has also suggested that advertisers, as well as media, risk reputational damage if native ads are thought to be deliberately deceptive (Darke 2007).
13 Since issuing the guidelines, the FTC has only once pursued enforcement for a native advertisement in an editorial publication, focusing instead on unclear labeling in social media. In early 2017, however, the head of the FTC Advertising Practices Division indicated that the agency was shifting its focus to publishers and brand studios (Steigrad 2017).
14 Virginia State Board of Pharmacy v. Virginia Citizens Consumer Council.

15 In January 2016, the British Advertising Standards Authority charged that a listicle in BuzzFeed UK, "14 Laundry Fails We've All Experienced," was not clearly identifiable as an ad. When BuzzFeed replied by pointing to several instances of labeling around the advertisement, the ASA insisted that the labels "did not, either in itself or in conjunction with the other page elements, adequately convey the commercial nature of the content to consumers. We therefore concluded that the ad was not obviously identifiable as such and that it therefore breached the Code."

## Bibliography

Aalberg, T. and Curran, J. eds. 2012. *How Media Inform Democracy: A Comparative Approach.* New York, NY: Routledge.

Allen, M., Azi, P. and Jimmy, V. 2014. "Capital Playbook: Vice Squeezed." Politico PRO, October 3, 2014. www.politico.com/states/new-york/albany/story/2014/10/capital-playbook-vice-squeezed-016309.

Amazeen, M. A. and Muddiman, A. R. 2018. "Saving Media or Trading on Trust? The effects of native advertising on audience perceptions of legacy and online news publishers." *Digital Journalism* 6, no. 2: 176–195.

An, S. and Bergen, L. 2007. "Advertiser Pressure on Daily Newspapers: A Survey of Advertising Sales Executives." *Journal of Advertising* 36, no. 2: 111–121.

Anderson, C. W. 2013. *Rebuilding the News: Metropolitan Journalism in the Digital Age.* Philadelphia: Temple University Press.

Anderson, C. W., Bell, E. and Shirky, C. 2012. *Post-Industrial Journalism: Adapting to the Present.* New York, NY: Tow Center for Digital Journalism.

Aribarg, A. and Schwartz, E. M. 2017. "Consumer Responses to Native Advertising." July 6, 2017. https://ssrn.com/abstract=2995467.

Baker, D. 2016. "Inside The Washington Post's Quest to Fix Ad Tech." *The Content Strategist*, October 6, 2016. https://contently.com/strategist/2016/10/06/ad-tech-washington-post/.

Bakir, V. and Barlow, D. M. 2007. *Communication in the Age of Suspicion: Trust and the Media.* Basingstoke, UK: Palgrave Macmillan.

Bakshi, A. C. 2015. "Why and How to Regulate Native Advertising in Online News Publications." *UB Journal of Media Law & Ethics* 4, no. 4: 4–47.

Basen, I. 2012. "Breaking Down the Wall." *Center for Journalism Ethics*, December 19, 2012. https://ethics.journalism.wisc.edu/2012/12/19/breaking-down-the-wall.

Battelle, J. 2014. "Programmatic Advertising's Audience Addiction." *Digiday*, May 27, 2014. https://digiday.com/media/programmatic-advertising-context/.

Beaujon, A. 2017. "The Washington Post's New Social Media Policy Forbids Disparaging Advertisers." *Washingtonian*, June 27, 2017. www.washingtonian.com/2017/06/27/the-washington-post-social-media-policy.

Beer, J. 2017. "A New Study Says Native Advertising Spend in U.S. to Reach $22 Billion This Year." *Fast Company*, March 21, 2017. www.fastcompany.com/3069121/a-new-study-says-native-advertising-spend-in-us-to-reach-22-billion-this-year.

Bell, E. 2014. "Native Advertising Is the New Paywall in Media Economics: But Is It Here to Stay?" *The Guardian*, January 5, 2014. www.theguardian.com/media/media-blog/2014/jan/05/native-advertising-paywall-transparency.

Benson, R. 2001. "Tearing Down the 'Wall' in American Journalism." *International Journal of the Humanities* 1: 102–113.

Benton, J. 2014. "Like It or Not, Native Advertising Is Squarely Inside the Big News Tent." *NiemanLab*, September 15, 2014. www.niemanlab.org/2014/09/like-it-or-not-native-advertising-is-squarely-inside-the-big-news-tent.

Better Business Bureau. 2016. "Native Advertising Added to BBB Code of Advertising; Deceptive Native Ads Now Violate the Code." *Better Business Bureau*, October 25, 2016. www.bbb.org/native-advertising-added-to-bbb-code-of-advertising/.

BI Intelligence. 2015. "Spending on Native Advertising Is Soaring as Marketers and Digital Media Publishers Realize the Benefits." *Business Insider*, May 20, 2015. www.businessinsider.com/spending-on-native-ads-will-soar-as-publishers-and-advertisers-take-notice-2014–11.

Blanchard, M. A. 1992. *Revolutionary Sparks: Freedom of Expression in Modern America*. New York, NY: Oxford University Press.

Boczkowski, P. J. 2004. *Digitizing the News: Innovation in Online Newspapers*. Cambridge: MIT Press.

Brants, K. 2013. "Trust, Cynicism and Responsiveness: The Uneasy Situation of Journalism in Democracy." In *Rethinking Journalism: Trust and Participation in a Transformed News Landscape*, edited by M. Broersma and C. Peters, 15–27. New York, NY: Routledge.

Brock, G. 2013. *Out of Print: Newspapers, Journalism and the Business of News in the Digital Age*. London: Kogan Page.

Calfee, J. E. and Ringold, D. J. 1988. "Consumer Skepticism and Advertising Regulation: What Do the Polls Show?" In *Advances in Consumer Research*. Vol. 15, edited by M. J. Houston, 244–248. Provo, UT: Association for Consumer Research.

Cameron, G. T., Ju-Pak, K.-H. and Kim, B.-H. 1996. "Advertorials in Magazines: Current Use and Compliance with Industry Guidelines." *Journalism & Mass Communication Quarterly* 73, no. 3: 722–733.

Cameron, G. T. and Curtin, P. A. 1995. "Tracing Sources of Information Pollution: A Survey and Experimental Test of Print Media's Labeling Policy for Feature Advertising." *Journalism & Mass Communication Quarterly* 72, no. 1: 178–189.

Cameron, G. T. 1994. "Does Publicity Outperform Advertising? An Experimental Test of the Third-Party Endorsement." *Journal of Public Relations Research* 6, no. 3: 185–207.

Cameron, G. T. and Haley, J. E. 1992. "Feature Advertising: Policies and Attitudes in Print Media." *Journal of Advertising* 21, no. 3 (September): 47–55.

Carlson, M. 2015. "When News Sites Go Native: Redefining the Advertising-Editorial Divide in Response to Native Advertising." *Journalism* 16, no. 7: 849–865.

Carr, D. 2013. "Storytelling Ads May Be Journalism's New Peril." *New York Times*, September 15, 2013. www.nytimes.com/2013/09/16/business/media/storytelling-ads-may-be-journalisms-new-peril.html.

Casale, A. J. 2015. "Going native: The rise of online native advertising and a recommended regulatory approach." *Cath. UL Rev.* 65: 129.

Chaffey, D. 2017. "Display Advertising Clickthrough Rates: Smart Insights Digital Marketing Advice." *Smart Insights*, January 31, 2018. www.smartinsights.com/internet-advertising/internet-advertising-analytics/display-advertising-clickthrough-rates/.

Chittum, R. 2014. "Native Ads: Advertorial for the Digital Age." *Columbia Journalism Review*, April 3, 2014. http://archives.cjr.org/the_audit/tpms_native_ads.php.

Christensen, C. 2015. "What Is Disruptive Innovation?" *Harvard Business Review*, December, 2015. www.ey.com/Publication/vwLUAssets/ey-hbr-disruptive-innovation/%24FILE/ey-hbr-disruptive-innovation.pdf.

Coddington, M. 2015. "The Wall becomes a Curtain: Revisiting Journalism's News-Business Boundary." In *Boundaries of Journalism: Professionalism, Practices and Participation*, edited by M. Carlson and S. C. Lewis, 67–82. New York, NY: Routledge.

Cole, J. T. and Greer, J. D. 2013. "Audience Response to Brand Journalism: The Effect of Frame, Source, and Involvement." *Journalism & Mass Communication Quarterly* 90, no. 4: 673–690.

Conill, R. Ferrer. 2016. "Camouflaging Church as State: An Exploratory Study of Journalism's Native Advertising." *Journalism Studies* 17, no. 7: 904–914.

Cookson, R. 2016. "News Media Move to Ban ad Blockers from Websites." *Financial Times*, July 6, 2016. www.ft.com/content/abf110aa-00b0-11e6-99cb-83242733f755?mhq5j=e1.

Cookson, R. 2015. "Watchdog Criticises Telegraph over Advertorial." *Financial Times*, December 29, 2015. www.ft.com/content/15b89176-ae3a-11e5-993b-c425a3d2b65a.

Critchlow, W. 2016. "A Checklist for Native Advertising: How to Comply with the FTC's New Rules." *Moz*, February 8, 2016. https://moz.com/blog/checklist-for-native-advertising.

Dahlen, M. and Rosengren, S. 2016. "If Advertising Won't Die, What Will It Be? Toward a Working Definition of Advertising." *Journal of Advertising* 45, no. 3: 334–345.

Darke, P. and Ritchie, R. 2007. "The defensive consumer: Advertising deception, defensive processing, and distrust." *Journal of Marketing Research* 44, no. 1: 114–127.

DeLorme, D. E. and Fedler, F. 2005. "An Historical Analysis of Journalists' Attitudes toward Advertisers and Advertising's Influence." *American Journalism* 22, no. 2: 7–40.

De Smet, D. and Vanormelingen, S. 2011. "Advertiser Pressure on Newspaper Journalists: A Survey." *Working Papers*. Hogeschool-Universiteit Brussel, Faculteit Economie en Management 37.

Deziel, M. 2016. "Why It's Time to Standardize Native Ad Labels." *The Content Strategist*, February 10, 2016. https://contently.com/strategist/2016/02/10/why-its-time-to-standardize-native-ad-labels.

Doctor, K. 2017. "Newsonomics: For the Newspaper Industry's Next Feat, Can It Get Donald Trump to Give It Antitrust Protection?" *NiemanLab*, July 17, 2017. www.niemanlab.org/2017/07/newsonomics-for-the-newspaper-industrys-next-feat-can-it-get-donald-trump-to-give-it-antitrust-protection/.

Domingo, D. and Paterson, S. eds. 2011. *Making Online News, Volume 2: Newsroom Ethnography in the Second Decade of Internet Journalism*. New York, NY: Peter Lang.

DVorkin, L. 2012. "Inside Forbes: The Birth of Brand Journalism and Why It's Good for the News Business." *Forbes*, October 3, 2012. www.forbes.com/sites/

lewisdvorkin/2012/10/03/inside-forbes-the-birth-of-brand-journalism-and-why-its-good-for-the-new-business/#330d223a93fd.

Eckman, A. and Lindlof, T. 2003. "Negotiating the Gray Lines: An Ethnographic Case Study of Organizational Conflict between Advertorials and News." *Journalism Studies* 4, no. 1: 65–77.

Edmonds, R. 2016. "A Look at Facebook's Billion Dollar 2016 Hit on the News Ecosystem." *Poynter*, November 30, 2016. www.poynter.org/news/look-facebooks-billion-dollar-2016-hit-news-ecosystem.

Edström, M., Kenyon, A. T. and Svensson, E.-M. eds. 2016. *Blurring the Lines: Market-Driven and Democracy-Driven Freedom of Expression*. Gothenberg: Nordicom.

Egan, B. D. 2017. "Can the Sanctity of Journalism be Maintained in an Era of Native Advertising? Case Study of Netflix." *Journal of Digital & Social Media Marketing* 4, no. 4: 339–351.

Einstein, B. R. 2015. "Reading between the Lines: The Rise of Native Advertising and the FTC's Inability to Regulate It." *Brooklyn Journal of Corporate, Financial, & Commercial Law* 10, no. 1: 225–248.

Einstein, M. 2016. *Black Ops Advertising*. New York, NY: Or Books.

Elkin, T. 2017. "Study Finds Two in Three Consumers Trust Branded Content More Than Traditional Advertising." *MediaPost*, June 21, 2017. www.mediapost.com/publications/article/303131/study-finds-two-in-three-consumers-trust-branded-c.html.

Ember, S. 2017. "New York Times Co. Reports Rising Digital Profit as Print Advertising Falls." *New York Times*, May 3, 2017. www.nytimes.com/2017/05/03/business/new-york-times-co-q1-earnings.html?_r=0.

Ember, S. 2015. "F.T.C. Guidelines on Native Ads Aim to Prevent Deception." *New York Times*, December 22, 2015. www.nytimes.com/2015/12/23/business/media/ftc-issues-guidelines-for-native-ads.html.

Erjavec, K. and Kovačič, M. P. 2010. "Relations with the Media: Who Are the Main Actors in an Advertorial Production Process in Slovenia?" *Journalism* 11, no. 1: 91–109.

European Union. 2006. "Directive against Misleading and Comparative Advertising." *European Union*, December 12, 2006. http://eur-lex.europa.eu/legal-content/EN/TXT/?uri=celex:32006L0114.

Federal Trade Commission. 2015a. "Enforcement Policy Statement on Deceptively Formatted Advertisements." *Federal Trade Commission*, 2015. www.ftc.gov/system/files/documents/public_statements/896923/151222deceptiveenforcement.pdf.

Federal Trade Commission. 2015b. "Native Advertising: A Guide for Businesses." *Federal Trade Commission*, December, 2015. www.ftc.gov/tips-advice/business-center/guidance/native-advertising-guide-businesses.

Federal Trade Commission. 2013. "Blurred Lines: Advertising or Content? An FTC Workshop on Native Advertising." *Federal Trade Commission*, December 4, 2013. www.ftc.gov/news-events/events-calendar/2013/12/blurred-lines-advertising-or-content-ftc-workshop-native.

Filloux, F. 2013. "Native Advertising: What's the Fuss?" *The Guardian*, April 22, 2013. www.theguardian.com/media/blog/2013/apr/22/native-advertising.

Fox, S. R. 1984. *The Mirror Makers: A History of American Advertising and Its Creators*. Chicago: University of Illinois Press.

Friestad, M. and Wright, P. 1994. "The Persuasion Knowledge Model: How People Cope with Persuasion Attempts." *Journal of Consumer Research* 21, no. 1: 1–31.

Funke, D. 2017. "What's behind the Recent Media Bloodbath? The Dominance of Google and Facebook." *Poynter*, June 14, 2017. www.poynter.org/2017/whats-behind-the-recent-media-bloodbath-the-dominance-of-google-and-facebook/463418.

Gallagher, K. 2017. "Programmatic Ad Buying Is Declining as Native Advertising Increases." *Business Insider*, July 11, 2017. www.businessinsider.com/programmatic-ad-buying-declining-native-advertising-increases-2017-7.

Gillespie, B. and Joireman, J. 2016. "The Role of Consumer Narrative Enjoyment and Persuasion Awareness in Product Placement Advertising." *American Behavioral Scientist* 60, no. 12: 1510–1528.

Goldstein, T. C. 2002. "Nike v. Kasky and the Definition of Commercial Speech." *Cato Sup. Ct. Rev.*: 63.

Goodman, E., Kurnit, R., Paioff, S., Sheff, J., Yi, P. and Wu, F. 2016. "Native Advertising." *Cardozo Arts & Entertainment Law Journal* 34, no. 3: 580–608.

Gottfried, R. A. 2015. "Six Ways This Article Is Most Definitely Not an Ad: Deceptive Marketing and the Need for Clearly-Defined Disclosure Rules in Online Native Advertisement." *Loyola Consumer Law Review* 27, no. 3: 399–422.

Greenslade, R. 2016. "Can Newspapers Do Anything to Stop the Advertising Exodus?" *The Guardian*, April 3, 2016. www.theguardian.com/media/2016/apr/03/advertisers-print-newspapers-adblocking.

Greenslade, R. 2012. "Media Lessons from Scandinavia: Where Press Self-Regulation Works." *The Guardian*, July 4, 2012. www.theguardian.com/media/greenslade/2012/jul/04/us-press-publishing-sweden.

Guardian News Media. 2015. "World's Leading Digital Publishers Launch New Programmatic Advertising Alliance, Pangaea." *The Guardian*, March 18, 2015. www.theguardian.com/gnm-press-office/2015/mar/18/worlds-leading-digital-publishers-launch-new-programmatic-advertising-alliance-pangaea.

Hajszan, C. 2016. "Is Native Advertising the Answer to Increasing Ad Avoidance?" *BrandBa.Se*, October 13, 2016. www.brandba.se/blog/2016/10/13/is-native-advertising-the-answer-to-increasing-ad-avoidance.

Hansen, T. 2017. "Why the Editorial Team Shouldn't Produce Native." *Native Advertising Institute*, August 29, 2017. https://nativeadvertisinginstitute.com/blog/editorial-team-native/.

Hindman, M. 2017. "Journalism Ethics and Digital Audience Data." In *Remaking the News: Essays on the Future of Journalism Scholarship in the Digital Age*, edited by P. J. Boczkowski and C. W. Anderson, 177. Cambridge: MIT Press.

Intel. n.d. "Polar Bears and Climate Change-Intel Drones Provide Answers." *Intel*. www.intel.com/content/www/us/en/technology-innovation/polar-bears-climate-change.html.

Interactive Advertising Bureau. 2015. "IAB Concerned about Guidance on Native Advertising." *IAB*, December 24, 2015. www.iab.com/news/iab-concerned-about-ftc-guidance-on-native-advertising/.

Interactive Advertising Bureau. 2013. "The Native Advertising Playbook." *IAB*, December 4, 2013. www.iab.com/wp-content/uploads/2015/06/IAB-Native-Advertising-Playbook2.pdf.

IPG Media Lab Team. 2016. "IPG Media Lab and Forbes Evaluate the Current State of Branded Content." *IPG Media Lab*, September 23, 2017. www.ipglab.com/2016/09/23/ipg-media-lab-forbes-evaluate-the-current-state-of-branded-content/.

Kafka, P. 2016. "Google and Facebook Are Booming: Is the Rest of the Digital Ad Business Sinking?" *Recode*, November 2, 2016. www.recode.net/2016/11/2/13497376/google-facebook-advertising-shrinking-iab-dcn.

Kent, T. 2017. "Advertising and News: Where's the line?" *Online News Association*. https://ethics.journalists.org/topics/advertising-and-news/.

Kim, B.-H., Pasadeos, Y. and Barban, A. 2001. "On the Deceptive Effectiveness of Labeled and Unlabeled Advertorial Formats." *Mass Communication & Society* 4, no. 3: 265–281.

Kirchner, J. 1986. "Advertorials Make Money, Stir Debate." *Advertising Age*: S17–S19.

Kreiss, D. 2016. "Beyond Administrative Journalism: Civic Skepticism and the Crisis in Journalism." In *The Crisis of Journalism Reconsidered: Democratic Culture, Professional Codes, Digital Future*, edited by J. C. Alexander, E. Butler Breese, and M. Luengo, 59–76. Cambridge: Cambridge University Press.

Krzeminska-Vamvaka, J. 2008. "Freedom of Commercial Speech in Europe." *Verlag Dr Kovac, Studien zum Völker- und Europarecht* 58: 292.

Kumar, V. and Gupta, S. 2016. "Conceptualizing the Evolution and Future of Advertising." *Journal of Advertising* 45, no. 3: 302–317.

Ladd, J. M. 2011. *Why Americans Hate the Media and How It Matters*. Princeton: Princeton University Press.

Laursen, J. and Stone, M. 2016. "Native Advertising Trends 2016: The News Media Industry." *Native Advertising Institute*, October, 2016. https://nativeadvertisinginstitute.com/wp-content/uploads/2016/10/TrendReportNewsMedia16.pdf.

Lazauskas, J. 2016. "Fixing Native Advertising: What Consumers Want from Brands, Publishers, and the FTC." *The Content Strategist*, 2016. https://contently.com/strategist/2016/12/08/native-advertising-study/.

Lazauskas, J. 2015. "Article or Ad? When It Comes to Native Advertising, No One Knows." *The Content Strategist*, September 8, 2015. https://contently.com/strategist/2015/09/08/article-or-ad-when-it-comes-to-native-no-one-knows.

Lepore, J. 2014. "The Disruption Machine: What the Gospel of Innovation Gets Wrong." *New Yorker*, June 23, 2014. www.newyorker.com/magazine/2014/06/23/the-disruption-machine.

Levi, L. 2015. "A 'Faustian Pact'?: Native Advertising and the Future of the Press." *Arizona Law Review* 57: 647–711.

Lewis, S. C. 2012. "From Journalism to Information: The Transformation of the Knight Foundation and News Innovation." *Mass Communication & Society* 15, no. 3: 309–334.

Liebes, T. and Ribak, R. 1991. "Democracy at Risk: The Reflection of Political Alienation in Attitudes Toward the Media." *Communication Theory* 1, no. 3: 239–252.

Lynch, J. 2015. "South Park Hysterically Satirized Ad Blocking and Sponsored Content." *Adweek*, November 19, 2015. www.adweek.com/tv-video/south-park-hysterically-satirized-ad-blocking-and-sponsored-content-168206/.

McChesney, R. W. and Pickard, V. eds. 2011. *Will the Last Reporter Please Turn Out the Lights: The Collapse of Journalism and What Can Be Done to Fix It*. New York, NY: New Press.

Madrigal, A. C. 2017. "The News Business Sinks Ever Closer to Rock Bottom." *The Atlantic*, July 10, 2017. www.theatlantic.com/technology/archive/2017/07/facebook-and-the-media/533079/.

Manjoo, F. 2017. "The Online Ad Industry Is Undergoing Self-Reflection: That's Good News." *New York Times*, April 5, 2017. www.nytimes.com/2017/04/05/technology/online-ad-industry-self-reflection.html.

Mitchell, A. 2014. "State of the News Media 2014." *Pew Research Center: Journalism & Media*, March 26, 2014. www.journalism.org/2014/03/26/state-of-the-news-media-2014-overview.

Mitchelstein, E. and Boczkowski, P. J. 2009. "Between Tradition and Change: A Review of Recent Research on Online News Production." *Journalism* 10, no. 5: 562–586.

Morrissey, B. 2017. "The New York Times CEO on State of Digital Advertising: 'Nightmarish Joke' – Digiday." *Digiday*, June 19, 2017. https://digiday.com/media/new-york-times-ceo-state-digital-advertising-nightmarish-joke/.

Mullin, B. 2015. "ASME Releases Guidelines for Native Advertising." *Poynter*, April 15, 2015. www.poynter.org/2015/asme-releases-guidelines-for-native-advertising/335937/.

Newman, N., Levy, D. A. and Nielsen, R. K. eds. 2015. "Reuters Institute Digital News Report 2015." *Reuters Institute for the Study of Journalism*. Oxford: University of Oxford.

Nielsen, R. K. 2016. "The Many Crises of Western Journalism." In *The Crisis of Journalism Reconsidered: Democratic Culture, Professional Codes, Digital Future*, edited by J. C. Alexander, E. Butler Breese, and M. Luengo, Cambridge: Cambridge University Press.

Petty, R. D. 1997. "Advertising Law in the United States and European Union." *Journal of Public Policy & Marketing* 16, no. 1: 2–13.

Pew Research Center. 2016. "State of the News Media: 2016." *Pew Research Center*, June 15, 2016. https://assets.pewresearch.org/wp-content/uploads/sites/13/2016/06/30143308/state-of-the-news-media-report-2016-final.pdf.

Ponkivar, A. B. 2015. "Ever-Blurred Lines: Why Native Advertising Should Not Be Subject to Federal Regulation." *North Carolina Law Review* 93, no. 4: 1187–1210.

Porlezza, C. 2017. "Under the Influence: Advertisers' Impact on the Content of Swiss Free Newspapers." *Media and Communication* 5, no. 2: 31–40.

Practical Law Company Magazine EU. 2012. "Misleading Marketing Practices: European Commission Adopts Communication on Review of Misleading and Comparative Advertising Directive." *PLC Law*, November 27, 2012. https://uk.practicallaw.thomsonreuters.com/3-522-7148?transitionType=Default&contextData=(sc.Default).

Rejón-Guardia, F. and Martínez-López, F. J. 2014."Online Advertising Intrusiveness and Consumers' Avoidance Behaviors." In *Handbook of Strategic e-Business Management*, edited by F. J. Martínez-López, 565–586. Heidelberg, Berlin: Springer.

Reuters Institute. 2017. "Reuters Digital News Report 2017." *Reuters Institute*, 2017. https://reutersinstitute.politics.ox.ac.uk/sites/default/files/Digital%20News%20Report%202017%20web_0.pdf.

Ryfe, D. M. 2016. *Can Journalism Survive? An Inside Look at American Newsrooms*. Cambridge: Polity.

Sahni, N. S. and Nair, H. S. 2016. "Native Advertising, Sponsorship Disclosure and Consumer Deception: Evidence from Mobile Search-Ad Experiments." *Federal Trade Commission*, February 23, 2016. www.ftc.gov/system/files/documents/public_events/966823/sahninair_native_advertisingsponsorshipdisclosureand consumerdeception.pdf.

Schauster, E. E., Ferrucci, P. and Neill, M. S. 2016. "Native Advertising Is the New Journalism: How Deception Affects Social Responsibility." *American Behavioral Scientist* 60, no. 12: 1408–1424.

Schudson, M. 1978. *Advertising, the Uneasy Persuasion: Its Dubious Impact on American Society*. New York, NY: Routledge.

Shinkevich, M. 2016. "'South Park' Lampoon of Native Advertising Highlights Important Issues." *Advertising Age*, February 24, 2016. http://adage.com/article/digitalnext/south-park-lampoon-native-advertising-highlights-issues/302756/.

Siles, I. and Boczkowski, P. B. 2012. "Making Sense of the Newspaper Crisis: A Critical Assessment of Existing Research and an Agenda for Future Work." *New Media & Society* 14, no. 8: 1375–1394.

Soley, L. C. and Craig, R. L. 1992. "Advertising Pressures on Newspapers: A Survey." *Journal of Advertising* 21, no. 4: 1–10.

Sonderman, J. and Tran, M. 2013. "Understanding the Rise of Sponsored Content." *American Press Institute*, November 13, 2013. www.americanpressinstitute.org/publications/reports/white-papers/understanding-rise-sponsored-content/single-page.

Starkman, D. 2013. "Native Ads' Existential Problem." *Columbia Journalism Review*, January 15, 2013. http://archives.cjr.org/the_audit/native_ads_existential_problem.php.

Steigrad, A. 2017. "The Federal Trade Commission to Scrutinize Media Companies." *WWD*, March 30, 2017. http://wwd.com/business-news/media/federal-trade-commission-to-crack-down-on-media-companies-native-advertising-10784810-10784810/.

Sullivan, M. 2015. "As Print Fades, Part 3: Sponsorships and Start-Ups." *New York Times*, September 28, 2015. https://publiceditor.blogs.nytimes.com/2015/09/28/as-print-fades-part-3-sponsorships-and-start-ups/.

Swant, M. 2016. "Publishers Are Largely Not Following the FTC'S Native Ad Guidelines." *Adweek*, April 8, 2016. www.adweek.com/digital/publishers-are-largely-not-following-ftcs-native-ad-guidelines-170705/.

Sweetser, K. D., Ahn, S. J., Golan, G. J. and Hochman, A. 2016. "Native Advertising as a New Public Relations Tactic." *American Behavioral Scientist* 60, no. 12: 1442–1457.

Tadena, N. 2014. "NYT Readers Spend Same Amount of Time on Paid Posts as News Stories." *Wall Street Journal*, May 14, 2014. https://blogs.wsj.com/cmo/2014/05/14/nyt-readers-spend-same-amount-of-time-on-paid-posts-as-news-stories/.

Taylor, C. R. 2017. "Native Advertising: The Black Sheep of the Marketing Family." *International Journal of Advertising* 36, no. 2: 207–209.

Urbanski, A. 2016. "67% of All Digital Ads Are Now Bought Programmatically." *DMN*, April 5, 2016. www.dmnews.com/digital-marketing/67-of-all-digital-ads-are-now-bought-programmatically/article/487766/.

Usher, N. 2014. *Making News at The New York Times*. Ann Arbor: University of Michigan Press.

Vinderslev, A. 2016. "The FTC's Latest Native Regulations: A Recap on the Debate That Followed." *Native Advertising Institute*, February 18, 2016. https://nativeadvertisinginstitute.com/blog/the-ftcs-latest-native-regulations-a-recap-on-the-debate-that-followed/.

Voorhees, J. 2013. "*The Atlantic* Yanks Scientology Advertorial After Outcry." *Slate*, January 15, 2013. www.slate.com/blogs/the_slatest/2013/01/15/the_atlantic_scientology_magazine_yanks_sponsored_content_after_outcry.html.

Wasserman, E. 2013. "Advertising Goes Native and Deception Runs Free." *Huffington Post*, April 1, 2013. www.huffingtonpost.com/edward-wasserman/native-advertising-atlantic-scientology_b_2575945.html.

Wemple, E. 2014. "John Oliver: Native Advertising Is 'Repurposed Bovine Waste'." *The Washington Post*, August 4, 2014. www.washingtonpost.com/blogs/erik-wemple/wp/2014/08/04/hbos-john-oliver-native-advertising-is-repurposed-bovine-waste/?utm_term=.5be95a35d91c.

White, I. 2016. "The Misconceptions, Benefits and Future of Native Advertising." *Affinio Blog*, September 20, 2016. www.affinio.com/blog/2016/09/20/interview-the-misconceptions-benefits-and-future-of-native-advertising-2/.

Wojdynski, B. W. 2016. "The Deceptiveness of Sponsored News Articles: How Readers Recognize and Perceive Native Advertising." *American Behavioral Scientist* 60, no. 12: 1475–1491.

Wojdynski, B. W. and Evans, N. J. 2016. "Going Native: Effects of Disclosure Position and Language on the Recognition and Evaluation of Online Native Advertising." *Journal of Advertising* 45, no. 2: 157–168.

# 2 Studio N

## In-house native advertising at US and European news publishers

This chapter documents the rise of in-house content studios at news outlets in the US, Europe, and elsewhere. I begin with an overall look at the phenomenon of the content studio; then, drawing on media coverage, scholarly research, and industry publications, I describe each studio's history and approach, providing examples of campaigns and clients. In some cases, I discuss how the content studio has catalyzed a larger transition at the outlet or reflect on what editors or publishers have said about native advertising as a phenomenon.

I have also tried to offer a cursory sense of the economic crises which have spurred the turn towards native advertising at many of these outlets, referring to posted or estimated losses. I foreground these finances here to emphasize that for many news outlets, the revenue from native advertising is a necessary, though not always sufficient, source of revenue for ailing companies: even if news outlets are profitable, it is often the case that it is their native advertising programs that are keeping them in the black. *BuzzFeed*, for example, which earns all of its revenue from native advertising, has been profitable since 2013.

As native advertising studios are evolving rapidly, this catalogue is by no means comprehensive, but it does present a fairly representative picture of how news outlets have embraced the idea of producing their own native content for advertisers, shifting from an arms-length relationship with those advertisers to a client or partnership relationship, and (in some cases), taking on all of the functions of a conventional advertising agency in the process.

### The birth of the "content studio"

In Chapter 1, I noted that while native advertising has deep roots in the news industry, including 19th-century "reading notices" and the op-ed advertorials published in national newspapers, the rise of the "content studio" or "brand studio" is a distinctly recent phenomenon. As the foregoing illustrates, online news outlets were the first news organizations to adopt native advertising, beginning with *BuzzFeed* in 2006. Many legacy outlets – such as *The New York Times* in the US and *El Pais* in Spain – were initially skeptical, if not disdainful, of native advertising, and came to it gradually because of advertiser demand (Sebastian 2013). In some cases, perhaps most notably (and disastrously) *The Atlantic*, initial forays into native advertising at news outlets preceded the emergence of content studios at news outlets; sometimes, as with *The Atlantic*, they also preceded any discussions between business and editorial about what native advertising partnerships might entail.

Between 2014 and 2016, however, legacy outlets rushed to create in-house content studios, and by the end of 2016 the presence of a brand or content studio seemed to be *de rigeur* at both online-only and legacy publications, whether that studio was effectively a two-person team mining a stable of freelancers or (as in the case of the *Times*) a global company with scores of employees. What these studios have in common is their separation from the editorial portion of the news outlet, though in practice that separation takes many forms. Sometimes the head of the content studio works closely with editorial to identify potential articles or pages for sponsorship, or timely topics that advertisers might want to address in native advertising. Sometime the staff the content studio works with includes freelancers producing content for both the studio and the editorial side of the paper. And sometimes a good number of the staff writers at content studios were formerly full-time editorial employees at the same news outlet, often reporters laid off because of financial troubles and rehired back into the advertising side of the paper. Though this cross-hiring between editorial and advertising would have been nearly unheard of even ten years ago, now it isn't uncommon.

Fraught as it may be, this almost-but-not-quite separation between content studios and editorial divisions is necessary for native advertising to work well. Ideally, native ads are not only topically consistent with a given news outlet, but also match the tone and style of the outlet's editorial output, so studios need to have writers on staff that are deeply conversant with the publications they work for. And the editorial division needs to know something about what the content division is doing, especially when sponsorship opportunities allow for the creation of editorial content that might have otherwise gone unwritten.

At some of these publications, however, the separation has almost entirely disappeared. At data-driven news outlets such as the *Washington Post*, the same algorithms that are used to generate ideas for editorial content are used to suggest topics to advertisers. At other places, like *Vice*, the chain of command ensures that decisions about native advertising are given equal weight – if not more weight – than editorial choices. And at many media outlets the "shiniest toys in the room" for storytelling, such as video and virtual reality production studios, exist because of their advertising potential, not their editorial potential.

Still, if lines are increasingly blurry behind the scenes, disclosure requirements for native advertising mean that there remains, for now, a visual separation between native advertising and editorial content. As I discuss in Chapter 1, this can take many forms: news outlets use markedly different strategies for labeling and display. For example, the *Wall Street Journal* usually uses a WSJ Custom Studios logo and a label that says "Sponsored Content: What's This?" with a link to a disclaimer; occasionally they also use the term "Partner Content." *Huffington Post* has a far more disorganized approach, in part because they have been doing native advertising for much longer: older native advertising content (2014–2015) is indexed in a special "Sponsored Content" section on the site, but individual articles are not always clearly labeled as sponsored content. Newer content is collected on an "@Sponsored" page; posts on this page are more clearly identified at the post level. The *Guardian* has been both careful and public about its labeling choices; in early 2016 the paper announced it would change the labels "sponsored by" or "brought to you by," to the phrases "supported by," and "paid content/paid for by," or "advertiser content/from our advertisers" as part of an effort to improve transparency (Bilton 2016). Disclosures for *New York Times* native advertisements have changed over time, but include the T Brand Studio logo, a "paid for and promoted by" notice in small type at the top of an article, and a small bottom slug announcing "The news and editorial staff of the *New York Times* had no role in this post's preparation."

Content studios also have different strategies for Search Engine Optimization (SEO), archiving, and bylining native articles. Some publications, such as *Quartz*, routinely delete old campaigns, leaving only a stub linked to the searchable URL. For the most part, however, content remains online; however, since it is rarely indexed with the rest of a news publication's content, it is difficult to find. As well, content studios rarely put datelines on native articles. This is understandable if you want a campaign to seem current, but it is sometimes almost impossible to determine when native campaigns have been published. *Politico* is a (welcome) outlier in this regard, as their campaigns generally have a dateline and a date in the article's URL. *Politico* also frequently bylines their native stories, another practice that has not been common in the industry thus far.

Aside from differences in labeling and attribution, in-house brand studios differ significantly in what kinds of advertisements they create. Native advertising, ideally, matches the tone of a publication and pitches to its target audience; beyond this, studios differentiate themselves with a focus on longform or shortform narratives; a commitment to infographics, visual storytelling, humor or whimsy; a primary focus on policy, lifestyle, or health; and the extent to which journalistic conventions (including bylines) appear as a feature of native content.

## Native advertising studios at US and Canadian legacy media outlets

### The New York Times

Since 1851, the *Times* has long set a global standard for quality reporting, a reputation it has maintained through the present despite a steady decline in print revenues. After a rocky transition into a digital-first production strategy, the paper has managed to stabilize through buyouts, layoffs and new revenue strategies, going from a $14 million loss in the first quarter of 2016 to a $13 million profit in the first quarter of 2017. In an interview, Times CEO Mark Thompson claimed that native advertising had helped to fuel a 19 percent growth in digital advertising during that time (Ember 2017). The *Times* now also has the second highest renewal rate in the industry: 71 percent (MediaRadar 2017).

Since officially launching the T Brand native advertising studio in 2014, the *Times* has produced a number of prominent campaigns that have successfully leveraged the newspaper's prestige to promote everything from computers to a new season of the Netflix series *Orange Is the New Black*. Even as the *Times* is slimming down its editorial, the T Brand Studio is growing, with over 100 employees and over 200 completed campaigns. It is also expanding globally; in 2016, the *Times* established T Brand International to create native advertising for global markets, with offices in London, Paris, and Hong Kong (Teicher 2016).

Though native advertising is now a powerful presence at the *Times*, its arrival has been met with trepidation and occasional resistance. In 2002, when the *Times* was still in the early stages of developing its online presence, the paper rejected an early effort at native advertising, a 2002 Sony campaign created by an external agency with the intention of closely resembling editorial content. Years later, when the paper first began considering a native advertising division, both the paper's media columnist and public editor wrote about their concerns. In 2013, then-executive editor Jill Abramson suggested that the Times would not embrace native advertising, as the practice could potentially dilute a news organization's editorial authority (Griffith 2013); the following year, her clash with Thompson over native was given as one of the reasons she was fired from her position (Auletta 2014).

Still, as the public editor noted, the *Times* (like many papers) had a history of creating editorial categories with an eye towards advertising relationships, such as the Circuits or Home section, as well as op-ed advertorials. The *Times* also experimented with sponsored content before 2014: for example, in the wake of the *Times'* much-lauded multimedia longform article "Snowfall," the paper published a similarly ambitious multimedia piece on horse racing, this time sponsored by BMW and featuring a prominent BMW logo placement in the navigation bar (Sebastian 2013). Though this sponsorship preceded the establishment of a native content division, similar sponsored profiles have since appeared as native advertising on the Times site, including a profile of dancers for the New York City Ballet sponsored by Cole Haan (T Brand Studio 2015).

Such profiles also typify the T Brand approach of creating "stories that influence the influential" (T Brand Studio 2017), or appealing to an elite demographic with well-reported stories focusing on affluent lifestyles. For example, a native campaign for Sotheby's described how to live "with and within art," showcasing art-filled homes that were being marketed as works of art themselves. Another campaign promoted Tropicana orange juice by writing about the "terroir" of juice, drawing an equation between mass-marketed juice and wine (T Brand Studio and Tropicana 2017).

Health is also a persistent focus. Phillips became an "official health partner" of the *Times* over a two-year period, running a series of health columns authored by T Brand Studio that garnered over 1.6 million page views; articles focused on sleep improvement, cardiac care innovation, air pollution, and smart toothbrushes. And (as I discuss more extensively in Chapter 3) the Studio has waded into policy territory as well, including articles on industrial innovation for GE (T Brand Studio and GE 2016), energy for Shell and Chevron, and farming for MilkPep, a milk advocacy group (T Brand Studio and MilkPep 2017). Perhaps the most well-known native piece produced by the *Times* – the Netflix promotion for *Orange Is the New Black* – explored the problems with women's prisons, an under-covered topic that the *Times* might not otherwise have written about (T Brand Studio and Netflix 2014).

Sebastian Tomich, senior Vice President for advertising and innovation at the *Times*, has been blunt about the *Times'* intention to shape T Brand Studio into an advertising agency that competed directly with the agencies that once had generated advertising content for the paper: he has been quoted as saying that it was "inevitable" that the *Times* would want to capture as much of a company's advertising dollar as possible. In preparation, the *Times* has acquired a virtual reality production house, an influencer marketing agency Hello Society, and the virtual reality studio FakeLove (Heine 2017). They have also been investing in creating native video content: in 2016, they created a video division called "The Selects" which matched well-known video producers with brands. In Chapter 4, former T Brand employee Ava Sirrah discusses T Brand in more detail, looking at how advertising strategy has evolved over time.

## The Wall Street Journal

The Rupert-Murdoch-owned *Wall Street Journal* resisted financial restructuring longer than most US newspapers, launching a 2020 plan in 2016 and beginning a round of layoffs in early 2017 (Gray 2017). The outlet has been pursuing native advertising as a revenue strategy since 2014, beginning with a "hybrid" native advertising project in which Adobe provided both underwritten and sponsored content on *CMO Today*, a separate WSJ-branded blog for marketing executives. By the end of the 2014, the *Journal* expanded their efforts and launched WSJ Custom Studio, a native studio similar to T Brand Studio with about 45 employees. In 2017, the *Journal* had the highest "renewal rate" in the industry, 73 percent (MediaRadar 2017).

Like the *Times*, the *Journal* has carried out ambitious campaigns for entertainment media companies, creating longform pieces intended to provoke interest in upcoming shows. For Netflix, WSJ Custom Studio produced an extended multimedia investigation into Pablo Escobar and the Medellin Cartel to promote the show *Narcos* (WSJ Custom Studio and Netflix 2015). The article – written in English and Spanish – was set in a scrolling layout that integrated text, video (some provided by Netflix) and a quiz. For a show about high-end escorts on the Starz network, the Studio created a somewhat shorter multimedia piece about the history of paid sex work titled "The Business of The Heart," using an economic focus to pitch the show to their readers (WSJ Custom Studio and Starz 2016).

One of the *Journal's* largest campaigns has been with Price Waterhouse Cooper, titled "Broader Perspectives: A Cybersecurity and Privacy Hub" (WSJ Custom Studio and PWC 2017), which features a series of articles on topics relevant to both companies ("How Businesses are Transforming Revenue Models by Monetizing – and Protecting – Customer Data") and individuals ("Your Child's Teddy Bear Could be Vulnerable to Hacking"). Other advertisements have included an article on "innovative" donut making meant to advertise "creative funding" at Chase Bank, and a long article about the future of sleep meant to promote flying business class at United Airlines.

## The Washington Post

*The Washington Post* opened its native advertising division, Brand Connect, in 2013 (later renamed Brand Studio), not long after the newspaper was purchased by digital tycoon Jeff Bezos. Currently, the Studio has about 50 staff members. Among the many changes Bezos made at the *Post* was to create an engineering team that worked for both the editorial and advertising divisions of the paper (Sloane 2016); as a result, the Studio uses the same multimedia longform template that the *Post* uses for its longform articles (Moses 2014). And like *Post* features, native ads use data and interactive graphics to make them more compelling, sometimes with a bit more playfulness than a standard editorial piece. For example, a native piece from SubZero on food waste features statistics on food waste that becomes visible as a user wipes away "refrigerator frost" with the cursor (WP Brand Studio and Sub Zero n.d.). Another longform piece from Phillips on the shift from service-based to "value-based" payments for healthcare was based on a survey of hospitals conducted jointly by the Post and Phillips and featured more than a dozen interactive data graphics (WP Brand Studio and Phillips 2017).

The *Post*'s native advertising division grew rapidly over the course of 2015 and 2016 as the paper's readership expanded during the 2016 Presidential campaign, and current national and international clients including Dell, GE, JP Morgan Chase, Siemens, UPS, Lockheed, Audi and FX show *The Americans*. In 2017, the *Post* had the fifth highest renewal rate in the industry, 66 percent.

Given its policy-minded demographic, the *Post* also runs native ads dealing with pressing policy issues. At first, the Studio used an advertorial approach, launching "Brand Connect Perspective" in 2014 to allow organizations to publish commentary in their opinion section, much like the *New York Times'* earlier advertorial program. But recently focus has shifted to producing policy content for clients. A recent campaign for the documentary *An Inconvenient Sequel* combined reporting on climate change with graphics suggesting action items for political engagement on the issue (WP Brand Studio and Paramount 2017).

One of the *Post's* most ambitious native pieces was an elaborate investigative article done for the Syfy Channel to promote their 2016 surveillance thriller *Hunters*, the channel's first effort at political drama. Titled "Shadow Mission," the Post piece surveyed US counter-terrorism and covert operations activities around the world by drawing on experts and former operatives, some of whom appear in short video interviews. This kind of in-depth reporting on American political activities has long been the hallmark of the *Post*, but unlike many of the *Post's* longform political investigations, "Shadow Mission" – despite the fact that the piece was exhaustively reported – was run without bylines, the authors identified only as "Staff Writers, WP Brand Studio" (WP Brand Studio and Syfy 2016).

In 2015, the *Post* began targeting readers with native advertising using an algorithm derived from its editorial recommendation system, Clavis.

The new algorithm, BrandConnect Intelligence, combined a user's browsing history with third-party data to serve online native ads to audience most likely to read them (Moses 2015). In 2017, a refined version of the algorithm served content to readers based not only on the topics they might be interested in, but on the kinds of multimedia they customarily engage with (Grinapol 2017). The new algorithm allowed readers to engage with select pieces of a longform native ad – or "Post Cards" – instead of the entire advertisement.

## The Boston Globe

The *Globe* began its *Boston Globe Insights* program in 2012, allowing small and medium sized businesses to write posts that appeared on *Boston.com*. Their native advertising division launched in 2015, when they hired a single "content specialist" to create BG Brand Lab. The Lab's first piece was a short profile of two business owners whose companies had been financed by Rockland Bank, a commercial bank in Massachusetts (BG Brand Lab and Rockland Bank 2015). Since then, they have produced a series of native longform pieces for clients, including a campaign for Pfizer called "Dear Scientist" in which a series of chronic disease patients "write" to scientists about their suffering and hope for a cure (BG Brand Lab and Pfizer 2017).

Initially, the *Globe*'s forays into native advertising were relatively modest, in part because the paper's owners had focused on generating revenue for the financially struggling paper through a high-priced subscription model (Van Zuylen-Wood 2017). But in 2016, the Brand Studio expanded with a new storytelling platform and a newly hired team of copywriters, designers, and editors; in 2017, the *Globe* has more than quadrupled the amount of campaigns produced by the Studio (Hansen 2017a).

## *Postmedia (Canada)*

Postmedia, a chain of newspapers that includes the *National Post*, *Financial Post*, and *Montreal Gazette*, was an early adopter of native advertising (which they initially described as "integrated advertising"). In 2012, The *Financial Post* launched *FP Energy*, a Shell-sponsored "national hub for news" on energy issues in Canada. In 2014, Postmedia launched a native advertising studio called Content Works, which works with a mainly freelance staff to produce content for Postmedia papers. One of the more successful ads from Content Works – a 2016 print, tablet, and video campaign for the *Montreal Gazette* on research programs at Concordia University – won an award from the International News Media Association and gained over 1.7 million impressions, a significant number for a regional Canadian newspaper (International News Media Association 2016).

## The Globe and Mail

Like the Postmedia papers, *The Globe and Mail*, Canada's "newspaper of record," has enthusiastically embraced native advertising. In 2014, it partnered with General Electric to launch a 90-day native advertising campaign featuring articles on business and innovation. After the success of the GE campaign, the *Globe* launched a native advertising division, now called the Edge Content Studio. The studio got off to a rocky start when a memo leaked indicating the *Globe* planned to rebrand their editorial staff as "content creators" who would be responsible for both editorial and native content. After meeting with resistance from the union, the plan was dropped (O'Berne 2014). Edge has produced work for both Canadian and international clients, including a campaign for Thompson Reuters that has run continuously at the paper since October 2014, producing over 70 articles looking at "how professionals can capitalize on great business opportunities" with the intention of bolstering Reuter's reputation within Canada.

## Native content studios at US legacy news magazines

Arguably, the changes in the media ecosystem have hurt news magazines even harder than daily papers; the ever-increasing pace of the news cycle has made their weekly format far less attractive to readers, and as the circulation of print editions of magazines has plummeted to the point of near-oblivion, newsstands and other public points of sale have begun to vanish across the US. Native advertising has thus had an obvious appeal for newsmagazines. Beyond the economic incentives, the newsmagazine format lends itself to the long-form native approach; magazines such as the *Atlantic* have produced exemplary native content that aligns closely with the publication's format and tone.

## The Atlantic

Only six years younger than *The New York Times*, *The Atlantic* magazine has been much nimbler in its transition to digital; recovering from a decade of solid revenue loss between 2000–2010, the magazine reinvented itself as a fresh online presence and became profitable, growing an audience far larger, younger, and more diverse than its previous print audience. After an early misstep with native advertising (the Scientology ad controversy described in Chapter 1), the *Atlantic's* Re:Think studio has become one of the most acclaimed native advertising departments in contemporary publishing, winning the lion's share of awards for its campaigns for national and international clients and earning more than 70 percent of the *Atlantic's* advertising revenue. Re:Think has a staff of 32 in the United States that produce up to six campaigns a month, and is opening up a UK-based global business team (Southern 2016a). In 2017, the *Atlantic* had the sixth-highest renewal rate in the industry, 64 percent, and the magazine is currently profitable and adding editorial staff (Sullivan 2017).

*The Atlantic's* 2017 marketing kit for Re:Think is clear about the continuity between the *Atlantic's* content and focus and the content created by Re:Think; it includes a timeline outlining key reporting in the *Atlantic's* 160-year history, declares that Re:Think shares the *Atlantic's* "philosophy for creating content" and "unique POV," and provides a calendar of issue topics, such as technology, health, and gender, so that possible advertisers can plan for native content that fits seamlessly into a given issue's theme (Atlantic Re:Think 2017).

Campaigns launched by the *Atlantic* over the past several years include a series for Jaguar on the British cultural influence on the US filmed with a 30-person crew in London (Elkin 2016); a series on how data is affecting various industries for IBM (Atlantic Re:Think and IBM 2016); and a long-form piece on American "first couples" created to promote the series *House Of Cards*. The *House of Cards* promotion, titled "The Ascent," features a timeline and images of actual American first couples along with a visualization of a language-processing analysis of the language of dominance and submission used by Claire and Frank Underwood, the first-couple protagonists of the television show (Atlantic Re:Think and Netflix 2016).

### Time *Magazine*

*Time*, launched in 1923, has struggled as its parent company, Time Inc., shifted its business from print to digital, and its future remains uncertain following the sale of Time Inc. to publishing powerhouse Meredith Corporation (Fuller 2018). The company posted a net loss of $28 million in the first quarter of 2017 and the company considered, then rejected, the idea of putting itself up for sale. *Time* itself has seen a substantial long-term decline in its print subscription numbers, and despite an early entry into the online space it has struggle to find a revenue model. As part of that effort, *Time* became serious about native advertising in mid-2014. Their decision reflected a historical embrace of sponsored content at *Time*, which, like the *New York Times*, ran a steady stream of advertorials from Mobil during the 1970s and 1980s. But it also marked a new chapter of how *Time* saw its relationship with advertisers; in 2014, incoming publisher Joe Ripp declared he had removed the "wall between church and state" that separated the advertising and editorial division, asking editors to report to the business side of the magazine and to occasionally help to create native content (Willens 2016). Ripp opened The Foundry, an in-house content production studio whose 125-plus members created native advertising and for all Time Inc. brands (including *Time* and *Fortune*) while also serving as a stand-alone advertising agency with clients such as Bank of America (Elkin 2016).

## Forbes

Founded in 1917 as an American business magazine, *Forbes* now generates 75 percent of its revenue from its online presence, relying on a small core staff and a network of over 1,500 freelancers to publish 300 to 400 stories a day (Takahashi 2015). In 2016, 35 percent of that advertising revenue came from native ads (Dvorkin 2016). *Forbes* does not have an extensive content production studio; instead, the magazine has focused on integrating brand-created content, introducing a program called AdVoice in 2010 that allowed advertisers to publish directly on the Forbes site. AdVoice was controversial at the time of its inception, but has persisted as a major revenue stream for Forbes (now called BrandVoice). On top of this, *Forbes* has been experimenting with what it describes as "co-storytelling," ad/content hybrids for mobile in which some content is produced by advertisers and some content is produced by the *Forbes* editorial staff (Horgan 2017).

## Native studios at US-based online-only news outlets

Online-only news outlets may be newer to the industry than legacy publications, but they are the first to adopt native advertising, and legacy news outlets have largely followed in their footsteps. Without the initial flush years of print advertising revenue to build their reputations and resources, online-only outlets have always had to innovate to find revenue sources: for some outlets, this meant building an entire publication around a native advertising model, while others continue to mix native advertising with digital display advertising.

### Huffington Post

In a field of rapidly expanding digital media empires, the *Huffington Post* remains a giant: over 800 employees publishing around 1,900 posts daily in 13 editions worldwide.

And from its inception in 2005, the *Huffington Post* has been a leader in developing revenue strategies for digital news; the site mastered SEO, focused on audience development, and used data to drive story placement long before other outlets got up to speed. Though much of that revenue has come from display advertising, the *Huffington Post* was an early innovator in native, launching its US-based "Partner Studio" in 2012. Their offerings have included lighter content – such as listicles or humorous graphics – shorter articles, often with a health/lifestyle emphasis on avoiding "travel madness" – and more serious work, such as a recent bylined, longform piece on energy and social change in Tanzania for the Caterpillar Foundation (Huffington Post and Caterpillar Foundation 2017.)

In part because of its long history with sponsored content and in part because of its chaotic editorial history, the *Huffington Post* has a mixed reputation when it comes to both church-state separation and the clear labeling of sponsored content. Though work is supposed to be produced by the Content Studio, the editorial staff has felt pressured to contribute as well; in early 2017 they unionized and ratified a contract that blocked them from working for the native division (Kelly 2017).

Recently, *Huffington Post* has become more ambitious about the idea of serving as a stand-alone advertising agency for its clients. In 2016, when the *Huffington Post* acquired the VR storytelling firm RYOT, the publication rebranded their advertising efforts under the RYOT Studio name (Confusingly, RYOT Studio currently serves at the in-house content agency for all of Oath, the current Verizon subsidiary that holds both AOL and Yahoo).

### BuzzFeed

Launched in 2006 by *Huffington Post* co-founder Jonah Peretti, *BuzzFeed* has become a global force, with 18 offices, 11 international editions, and seven billion site views a month (Bennett 2017). Though it still faces reputational challenges – indeed, it has often been described as "an advertising agency that creates content" (Goefron 2015) – in the past few years it has been increasingly producing journalism of interest, and Peretti now considers serious journalism to be a core part of the site's mission (Peretti 2015). If *BuzzFeed* is an advertising agency, it has been a fairly successful one, and as a result it has been able to hire high-profile journalists from outlets such as *Politico*, *The New York Times*, and *ProPublica*.

*BuzzFeed's* success in advertising is in part due to Peretti's decision to eschew display advertising entirely, forgoing banner ads and pop-ups in favor of a native-only strategy. Unlike legacy news sites, *BuzzFeed's* native advertising is not meant to draw on the site's prestige or reputation, but rather to capitalize on *BuzzFeed's* ability to use data science to make its native content viral on social media. Typical native ads for *BuzzFeed* are not longform investigations or "think" pieces, but humorous quizzes, listicles, or short videos that are scarcely distinguishable from *BuzzFeed's* other editorial content. Working with Intel, for example, *BuzzFeed* created a nostalgic listicle about soon-to-be-extinct learning technologies such as blackboards and overhead projectors (BuzzFeed and Intel 2014).

Though their financial success has been an inspiration for other outlets pursuing native advertising, *BuzzFeed* has made several missteps over the years. In 2013, *BuzzFeed* partnered with *The Economist* to create a native ad for that publication, which resulted in a listicle that used a series of somewhat inane gifs to draw attention to reporting at the *Economist*. The tone-deaf listicle has since shown up on several "worst native advertising" lists (Wiser 2013). In 2015, the publication was criticized for overly cozy advertising-editorial relations when content critical of Dove and Hasbro was deleted after *BuzzFeed* signed both for native campaigns (Trotter 2015). As I discuss in Chapter 4, *BuzzFeed* has also drawn criticism for soliciting native advertising from political candidates during the 2012 and 2016 election.

## Quartz

A spin-off from *The Atlantic* in 2012 that was intended as a born-digital American analog to the *Economist* (Moses 2016), *Quartz* caters to affluent, professional readers searching for well-written business analysis as well as quick, elegant summations of news. It has been remarkably successful building a revenue model based entirely on digital advertising, and native content has been key to that success (Flamm 2017). *Quartz* has a ten-member native advertising division, Quartz Bulletins, that produces well-written, complex content much like *The Atlantic's* Re:Think Studio. And like *The Atlantic*, *Quartz* has been quite successful; currently, about 33 percent of *Quartz's* revenue comes from native content.

Examples of Quartz Bulletins include an advertisement for Siemens describing how the company is using data to reduce traffic (Quartz Bulletins and Siemens 2015) and a detailed infographic showing GE's contributions to industrialization (Maerkl 2015). For The Bank of America, *Quartz* has produced a yearly series of graphics and articles summarizing topics discussed at the World Economic Forum in Davos, written in real time by the *Quartz* native team. The Bank of America content, labeled as sponsored content, typically runs alongside coverage of Davos produced by the *Quartz* editorial team.

Though it caters to a different audience, *Quartz*, like *BuzzFeed*, was conceived from the beginning as a vehicle for digital advertising, and its publishers have focused on creating ads and content optimized for the interests and consumption patterns of its readers. This means well-written analytic content that is relatively short, and highly visual so as to be optimized for mobile viewers. In 2016, *Quartz* had the third-highest renewal rate in the industry, 69 percent (MediaRadar 2017).

## Politico

Founded in 2007 by former *Washington Post* staffers, *Politico* has grown into one of the most influential political voices in the US, with nearly 500 employees, over eight million monthly visitors and an estimated annual revenue of $80 million (Uberti 2016). Though much of *Politico's* business model revolves around paid subscriptions for "pro" content aimed at Washington insiders, the company turned to native advertising in 2013 as a means of drawing advertisers to its policy-focused audience. After initially publishing editorial-style content produced by brands or agencies, *Politico* opened an in-house studio in 2015 called Politico Focus (Raudenbush 2015). With a staff of about 15 and a large pool of freelancers, Politico Focus produces long-form sponsored content focused on policy issues that rival native advertisements produced by legacy outlets in their length and complexity. In 2015 and 2016, *Politico* began experimenting with sponsored advertising for political candidates, and in 2015, *Politico* opened a European edition and began working with European native advertising clients.

According to Politico Focus head Nick Yeager, *Politico*'s issue-focused native advertising needs to accomplish one of five specific goals:

> [It] must be useful in terms of helping people do their jobs better; involve accountability journalism (Yeager points to a Trump campaign); stadium moments (based on a theory that Politico's niche audience imbibes big "tune-in" moments in politics in the same way that fans engage with big sporting events like the Super Bowl); community journalism (which looks at topics and issues that impact specific communities); and ideas-based journalism (examining bigger themes that are driving policy discussions and the advocacy of ideas).
>
> (Elkin 2016)

One example of *Politico*'s "ideas-based journalism" approach to native content is a piece on the role of bleach in fighting Ebola produced for the American Chemistry Council; the article ran almost to 2,000 words and included video, audio, and interactive graphics (Politico Focus and American Chemistry Council 2015). Another article on the recovery of Detroit – for JP Morgan Chase – ran close to over 1,600 words, and featured interactive graphics and slideshows mapping out Detroit's revitalization. It was credited to Allison Arieff, "a contributing Politico Focus writer covering urban infrastructure and revitalization." The byline suggested the value placed on the journalists producing native work; in this case, the writer's particular expertise (Politico Focus and JP Morgan Chase 2017).

## Axios

*Axios*, founded in 2015 by former *Politico* staffers, is one of the most recent US news upstarts to embrace native advertising; in fact, the site's founders announced that their intention was to "fix" native advertising with the Axios format. This "fix" involves a rejection of the elaborate, longform native content produced by content studios in favor of brief in-feed messages that often link to external documents or websites. Most clients are brand or policy-focused, including the American Petroleum Institute, Goldman Sachs, and the Saudi Government.

## Vox

The news site *Vox* is owned by Vox Media, a company that also oversees niche sites including *The Verge, Recode*, and *Eater*. In the past few years, *Vox* has grown rapidly, with current traffic inching closer to sites such as the *Huffington Post* and *BuzzFeed*. Vox Media coordinates native advertising on all platforms through their VoxCreative division, launched in 2013. Its native advertising program has been less prominent than the efforts of some of its competitors, though recent ad-sharing agreements with NBC and Conde Nast – and the hiring of a COO to oversee native advertising – will probably increase the quantity of native advertising on the sites. *Vox* sponsored content for food, sports, and other lifestyle clients, much of which is clearly labeled. However, in some cases, content is written in-house before advertisers are approached, and the labeling is less clear. For example, a "partner" piece on innovation in Kansas City that was written and then presented to Ford as an opportunity for video advertising. Though Ford was identified as a sponsor in the video portion of the ad, the text article on Kansas City had no labeling (Sonderman and Tran 2013).

## Slate

*Slate* began what they described as an "embedded publishing" program in 2012 (Bilton 2014b), later launching an in-house content division called Slate Custom. Currently, the publication gets over half of its revenue from native advertising, and in 2016 Slate Custom was restructured into a 13-member native advertising team with the mandate of making advertising align more closely with the "editorial DNA" of *Slate* (Moses 2016). Recent efforts along those lines have included an interactive graphic on smart cities for Siemans (SlateCustom and Siemens 2016), and an ongoing series of "good news" stories sponsored by Wells Fargo, including a story on beatboxing at a school for the blind and one on the connection between individual acts and viral social movements (Slate Custom and Wells Fargo 2012).

## Vice

Like *BuzzFeed, Vice* has evolved into a global content company with an expanding news division, though the path to its present iteration was far more complicated. Starting as a subculture print monthly in Canada in the mid-1990s, *Vice* moved to the US as a print and web operation, then later opened outposts in Britain and elsewhere. Now largely video-driven, *Vice* has gradually shifted from covering mainly pop culture to covering hard news, sometimes finding themselves criticized for their sensationalistic approach. Their news division, *Vice News*, was launched in late 2013, producing documentary-style news video and web content, including an Emmy-Award winning series for HBO.

According to co-founder Shane Smith, *Vice*'s expansion has been funded, in large part, by native advertising; indeed, the company grew exponentially as a result of a $40 million native advertising deal with Intel in 2009. As Smith explained in a 2016 *Quartz* interview, *Vice* produced a series for Intel called *The Creator's Project*:

> That program built the company. You learn, holy shit, we could do a $40 million deal with Intel where we actually create content that we like, and they don't give notes! Why were we doing banner ads? Those $40 million deals have turned into $100 million deals.
>
> (Rodriguez 2016)

Smith's philosophy of advertising is similar to *BuzzFeed's*: he has argued that both publishers and brands need to adapt to a near-future world without display advertising, in which "content partnerships" are the primary means of publicity and revenue (Bacon 2016). This focus on "partnerships" rather than campaigns also reflects Smith's belief that brands need to think of themselves as media producers or co-producers (Robischon 2016) Currently, the company gets about half of its revenue from native advertising in print and video (Hagey 2016). Their native ads reflect *Vice's* focus on politics and entertainment and their ability to attract a younger audience; for example, recent web projects included a series exploring perceptions of refugees that was created in partnership Western Union (Vice and Western

Union 2016; Vice and Western Union 2017), and a campaign for Smirnoff on gender equality in music (Vice and Smirnoff 2017).

As more and more of its audience shifts to mobile, *Vice* has struggled with renewal rates for native advertising; as a result, they have created an 30-person in-house team, Vice Labs, to work on text and video mobile campaigns and to develop native advertising for *Viceland*, Vice's new cable television program (Joseph 2016). In 2017, they hired a research firm to study the effectiveness of their text and video native advertising. They also expanded their advertising services, creating the agency Virtue Worldwide.

Though Smith has claimed that *Vice* has editorial independence even when it comes to sponsored video content (Swaine 2014), former *Vice* staffers have claimed that the company had been known to kill stories that might antagonize their brand partners (Sterne 2014; Lytvynenko 2015).

## Native content studios at European and UK legacy media

### The Guardian

Over the past decade, the British-based *Guardian* has emerged as one of the key players in the online news industry, winning accolades for its digital innovation and design as well as its reporting. In 2011 and 2013 it expanded its purview, opening "Guardian US," "Guardian Australia," and "Guardian International" sites. In 2012, it ranked as the third most-read newspaper website globally (Stipp and GNM Press Office 2012), attracting an educated, liberal, and cosmopolitan audience. Much of the transformation took place under the leadership of former editor Alan Rusbridger, who, like then Director General of the BBC John Birt, became convinced of the need for an aggressive approach to moving online after a visit to Silicon Valley in the mid-1990s (Kung 2015).

Like most news brands, the *Guardian* continues to struggle financially. Though the paper has been sustained since the 1930s by the Scott Trust, recent operating losses have totaled from 70–100 million pounds a year and threatened to drain the Trust's financial reserves (Williams 2017). Preferring to control costs rather than establish a paywall or subscription model (Murrell 2016), the paper has gone through several rounds of redundancies, including 300 staff in 2016. This means that – again, like most news outlets – the *Guardian* has been downsizing its editorial staff at the same time that it tries to expand its native advertising offerings.

The *Guardian* created an in-house content studio, Guardian Labs, in 2014, as a means to "work with companies to create marketing campaigns that go beyond buying advertising space online in the newspaper" (Sweney 2014).

The Labs have grown to over 130 staff members, including designers, video producers, writers, and brand strategists. Their native output falls into three categories: underwritten content produced by the editorial division, content produced on behalf of a client by the Labs, and content supplied directly by the advertiser, which is now placed in a special "hosted" section of the website.

Content produced by Guardian Labs is elaborate and ambitious, and is consistent with the Guardian's own focus on science, politics and culture. For the car manufacturer Seat, the *Guardian* produced a multimedia piece profiling innovators which allows the user to choose an audio or text stream to navigate the content and a short film on brain activity and romantic love (Guardian Labs and Seat 2016). For technology company Vulcan, the *Guardian* spent 12 months researching elephant conservation, and subsequently wrote a longform piece that explored conservation and poaching (Guardian Labs and Vulcan 2016). For Cisco, the Labs produced an interactive exploring the Internet of Things (Guardian Labs and Cisco 2015). The *Guardian* also has underwriting partnerships with a number of British and international foundations, including the British Academy, The Woodland Trust, and the Rockefeller Foundation.

### The Economist

*The Economist* has a long history of working directly with advertisers; their Economist Intelligence Unit dates back to 1946 (Sternberg 2012). In 2013, the publication added a 14-person content marketing unit, but they often use native advertising as part of a larger campaign that might include whitepapers, events, and research surveys produced by *Economist* staff. Examples include a series on technology and business for Microsoft, a partnership with GE that included a GE-branded section on innovation (*Look Ahead Powered by GE*) and a three-year sponsorship of a separate *Economist* blog (*The Economist Explains*). Like Shane Smith of *Vice*, the *Economist's* digital strategy head has predicted that display advertising will disappear in the near future, though he is skeptical that native advertising will replace the lost revenue (Standage 2016).

### Financial Times *(Britain)*

The *Financial Times* created its native advertising division, FT Squared, in late 2015. Like the *Guardian*, they have editorially produced content that is underwritten – such as a series on "distinctive living" sponsored by Sotheby's – as well as content produced by FT Squared. Examples of FT Squared campaigns include an exploration of aging for Auriens (FT Squared and Auriens 2017) and an infographic on the history of luxury air travel for

VistaJet. (FT Squared and VistaJet 2017). *The Financial Times* has been relatively cautious about native advertising, and editors maintain that they have final say over all content – whether editorial or native (Davies 2015).

## The Telegraph

The British *Telegraph* launched its content division, Spark, in early 2015, focusing mainly on sports, travel and lifestyle clients. Spark's native ads are simple – games, quizzes, and short articles including texts and images a standard web layouts – though a recent campaign included a simple interactive map of Flanders on behalf of the Flanders tourism bureau (*Telegraph* and Flanders Tourism 2012). Notably, the *Telegraph* has faced criticism both for its native advertising labeling practices (Jackson 2015) and the alleged spiking of critical stories about advertisers (Oborne 2015).

## Schibsted *(Norway and Sweden)*

*Schibsted*, which publishes newspapers such as *Verdens Gang* and *Aftenposten* in Norway and *Aftonbladet* in Sweden, gets a large portion of revenue from classified advertising, but it has been trying to make inroads into native advertising in a region notably more averse to the format. In 2015, the publishing group increased their native advertising efforts; instead of creating a separate content studios, however, *Aftonbladet* and *VG* reorganized their newsrooms into three editorial units: one focusing on breaking news events, another on investigative journalism, and a third entirely focused on paid content (*Schibsted* 2015).

The response to these changes have been mixed; *Verdens Gang*, in particular, has been criticized by the Norwegian Press Complaints Commission for misleading advertising. (Schibsted Media Group 2016). At the same time, VG received recognition from IMNA for a long-form native article on the 1934 Tajford landslide and tsunami to promote Nordisk Films' *The Wave*. The article, written by a well-known Norwegian journalist and featuring historical photos and graphics connected to the disaster, received 300,000 hits in the first 36 hours, an impressive audience for a Norwegian news site (Schibsted Brand Studio 2016).

## *Independent News and Media (Ireland)*

Independent News and Media, owned by Irish billionaire Denis O'Brien, publishes Ireland's most-read newspaper the *Irish Independent*, along with the *The Herald, Sunday World, Belfast Telegraph, Sunday Life, Star*, and a number of regional papers. INM launched its in-house studio, StoryPlus, in 2015, with eight staff members and about a dozen freelancers (Hansen 2017b). StoryPlus produces multimedia content in health, travel, and lifestyle clients; examples include a profile of creatives in Irish advertising for Mini Cooper and a tour of Irish Big Houses for the Irish Tourist Board (StoryPlus and Ireland's Ancient East 2017).

## The Irish Times

*The Irish Times*, Ireland's second-largest newspaper, has been struggling financially due to circulation declines, reporting an operating loss of more than a million Euros in 2015 (Boland 2017). In addition to placing its content behind a paywall, the *Times* has been developing native advertising since 2016 through the Irish Times Content Studio, focusing mainly on financial and lifestyle advertising for clients such as Samsung, Bushmills, and Ulster Bank. Steering away from data and interactivity, the Content Studio produces articles that often include short, well-produced introductory videos and focus on individual stories. A 2016 campaign, a profile of the Irish Olympic swimmer Nuala Moore done for Audi, won the 2017 INMA Global Media award for Best Execution of Native Advertising (*Irish Times* and Audi 2017).

## *BBC*

Though BBC's British broadcasting operations are advertisement free – at least until 2027, when the BBC charter is up for renewal – it began running advertisements on the BBC website outside the UK in 2007 (Sweney 2012). In 2015, to bring native advertising to these sites, the BBC launched StoryWorks, a global content studio with offices in the US, UK, Singapore, and Australia. StoryWorks describes itself as "the premier creative studio with newsroom values that carry the BBC's mark of quality" (BBC 2017). The content studio coordinates the production of digital and video advertisements of three distinct types: "partnered content" produced by the StoryWorks division that is paid for by a brand but not brand-specific; "advertisement features" which are created by StoryWorks and specifically promote advertisers; and "sponsored content" which is paid for the advertiser but created by an independent editorial team. Examples include an article about hiking in Quebec produced for Quebec Tourism that appeared in BBC Travel (BBC World and Quebec Travel 2015), a series of profiles of British scientists and philanthropists for the car company Skoda (BBC StoryWorks and Skoda 2016), and a video profile of a blind painter and others who have "achieved against all odds" for the IT company Huwei (BBC StoryWorks and Hauwei 2017).

In an effort to prove the effectiveness of its native content and the role played by labeling, the BBC conducted a facial-tracking study in 2016 on order to measure audience responsiveness to ads, claiming that the study showed that BBC native advertising was as trusted and persuasive as editorial content, especially when well labeled. A subsequent study suggested that most native advertising produced an emotional response from the viewer – even if the emotion produced was sadness or anger (Davies 2016b). At the time, StoryWorks was said to be responsible for 30 percent of all BBC advertising sales (Davies 2016a).

## Native studios at online-only European news outlets

### *Burda Forward*

Burda Forward is Germany's largest content studio, creating native advertising for *Huffington Post Germany, FOCUS Online*, and a number of other sites that collectively reach about 60 percent of the German media audience. Their portfolio is similar to that of Huffington Post Studio; mostly short and medium-length text pieces in standard web formats, enhanced with video and slideshows and the occasional quiz or interactive graphic. Clients are mainly finance, health, and lifestyle-related and include Brita, Bayer, and Deutsche Bahn. Presently, native advertising supplies between 15 and 50 percent of the revenue for their client sites (Notting 2016). Burda Forward's approach is to think of editorial and marketing as a collective endeavor, which means that their native content should work as a form of editorial content, providing "news and services" to their audiences instead of being product-focused (Notting 2016). Much of their native content does resemble service journalism, though products are prominently mentioned in many ads.

### *RCS Studio (Italy)*

RCS Media, publisher of Corriere Della Sera, Italy's second most-read news website, and other papers and magazines, began experimenting with native advertising in 2014 and founded RCS Studio in 2015; currently they are a branch of the RCS advertising division and have a staff of 11 (Hansen 2017c). Native advertising has been slow to develop in Italy, and RCS gives final control over native content to the editor of each publication and ensures "church-state" separation, meaning that most native content is written by freelancers. RCS creates both short and long-form native contents, sometimes accompanied by live events. Examples include a "Change is Good" campaign for Hyundai that focuses on embracing the concept of change, and a longform piece on innovation in Italy for the Italian department store Rinascente that included an exhibition at the Palazzo de Real (RCS 2015, 2017).

## Meduza *(Latvia/Russia)*

*Meduza* is a Russian-language news outlet based in Latvia that describes itself as "Russia's free press in exile" (Tomkiw 2015). It has a primarily Russian readership of about seven million unique visitors a month. *Meduza* embraced native advertising from the beginning, and has worked with lifestyle and entertainment clients including Airbnb, eBay, and Netflix (Hansen 2017d); they frequently create campaign featuring games and other forms of interactivity. In 2015, *Meduza* published a lengthy statement of principles for native advertising on the publication's *Medium* channel. *Meduza's* editor argued that the production of native advertising should be kept separate from editorial production, though its conception should be the responsibility of the editorial team as well as the advertising team, in order to "strengthen the advertising portion of the publication with editorial expertise." He also noted that "serious" native content – longform reporting on behalf of a brand – needs to be extremely selective and subject to final review by the publication's editor (*Meduza* 2015).

## Helsingin Sanomat

Though (like other Finnish newspapers) *Helsingin Sanomat* is partly supported by the Finnish government (Reunanen 2017), it has been struggling financially due to declining circulations. Along with establishing a paywall, *HS* has been slowly experimenting with native advertising, working with the content marketing division of parent company Sanoma Media to develop campaigns for financial, lifestyle, and advocacy clients. Some of these experiments have involved coordination with editorial; for example, *HS* used the publication's proprietary data journalism tools to create visualizations of company data on Finland's auto accident trends in a high-profile campaign for the Nordic insurance company IF (Laursen and Stone 2016, 13). Following the success of that campaign, HS coordinated with IF on similar data dives, including a campaign on Finnish property crime (Korhonen 2016).

## El Pais

*El Pais*, Spain's largest paper, has been slow to embrace online advertising due to the legacy outlet's concerns about breaking down walls between business and editorial (Southern 2016b). But the paper is quickly transitioning to digital-first, and as part of that process has engaged in some significant partnerships, including a campaign with Vodafone featuring a series of interview with innovators such as the founder of the Internet Archive and the creator of Tor (*El Pais* and Vodafone n.d.).

Much of *El Pais'* native advertising innovation takes place on *Verne*, an online spinoff of *El Pais* launched in 2014 and aimed at attracting younger readers through viral content. *Verne* runs a mix of advocacy and lifestyle advertising aimed at younger audiences, all of which are marked as "contenido patrocinado" but not often brand-identified. For example, a sponsored article on air conditioning and conservation featured a video advertisement for a recycled flip flop but no clear indication that the brand was the sponsor (Verne and Ecoalf 2015).

### *The* Times of India

The *Times of India* is owned by the media conglomerate Bennett, Coleman and Company, run by Samir and Vinet Jain, media executives legendary for their disregard for the wall between advertising and editorial (Auletta 2012). The *Times* has had an in-house content studio since 2003, when it established Medianet to provide what it labeled "advertorial" content (Anderson, Williams and Ogola 2013, 275) in supplements to the main paper. The *Times* justified the move as a means to "capture content from outside conventional news sources" while serving the role of "conscience-keeper, auditor and watchdog, regulating the media's burgeoning interaction with the PR sector" (*Times of India* 2003). Medianet has been highly lucrative for the *Times*, but it has also attracted a good deal of criticism for poor labeling and lack of editorial filter. In 2010, the Indian Press Council claimed that Medianet's practices led to the widespread implementation of paid coverage in regional and national newspapers during Indian elections (Sainath 2010). The *Times* has also engaged in in-house advertorial production; these ads are usually articles written by staff writers and are minimally labeled (Auletta 2012).

## Conclusion: studio N?

As the studio profiles in this chapter attest, native advertising studios have become a common (if not near-ubiquitous) revenue source at legacy and online-online media outlets around the world. In most cases, these brand or content studios are as unique as the publications they support. However, some studios support multiple publications and others (a rare few) are beginning to produce content for clients that can be used wherever the client chooses: in other words, content that has the appearance of native advertising but the portability of conventional display advertising. The latter development is one indicator that some brand studios have recently begun to think of themselves as less the advertising arm of a given publication and more the stand-alone ad agencies serving as the "agency of record" for a stable of permanent clients. This development is not surprising, given the talent hired by top studios and the high-profile campaigns they undertake. These studios are clearly headed for a collision course with the rest of the advertising world, and it is unclear how that conflict will reshape both industries.

However this conflict plays out, it is probably also the case that the lion's share of the studios described here will not embrace these larger ambitions, and will instead focus on creating purpose-built advertising campaigns for clients who wish to appeal to their publication's particular audience. This does not mean that they will not evolve significantly; given how new many of these studios are, we should expect radical changes in how native campaigns are authored and labeled as media audiences, media executives, and media regulators weigh in on the effectiveness of native content. Hopefully, these changes will be largely positive. For example, emerging standards around native advertising might help tighten lax labeling rules at places such as the *Times of India* (where native advertising is essentially the same as pay-to-play journalism), and industry conversations about failed or successful campaigns might provide a better "playbook" for studios trying to design labor-intensive individualized campaigns.

The question remains, however: what does success look like for these studios? Many are growing aggressively, in an environment in which digital display advertising is less and less important to the bottom line of their home publications. What happens if *all* publications become native-only, if all advertising is narrative, if news outlets are staffed by two equally sized and resourced writing teams, one with an advertising function and one with an editorial function? Is such a vision even possible, given that the market for native advertising remains a niche market with a select group of clients and a unique set of goals? Perhaps more importantly: is it desirable, or do some of the concerns raised in Chapter 1 become more pressing if native advertising continues its current rate of growth? In the next chapter, I look at one area of native advertising whose growth raises a particular set of concerns about journalism and democracy: native advertisements whose intent is not brand advocacy, but issue advocacy.

## Bibliography

Allen, M., Paybarah, A. and Vielkind, J. 2014. "Capital Playbook: Vice Squeezed." *Politico PRO*, October 3, 2014. www.politico.com/states/new-york/albany/story/2014/10/capital-playbook-vice-squeezed-016309.

Anderson, P. J., Williams, M. and Ogola, G. eds. 2013. *The Future of Quality News Journalism: A Cross-Continental Analysis*. Vol. 7. New York: Routledge.

Atlantic Re:Think Marketing Information. 2017. *The Atlantic*. https://advertising. theatlantic.com/rethink.

Atlantic Re:Think and IBM. 2016. "Augmenting The Way We Think." *The Atlantic*. www.theatlantic.com/sponsored/ibm-2016/augmenting-the-way-we-think/798/.

Atlantic Re:Think and Netflix. 2016. "The Ascent." *The Atlantic*. www.theatlantic. com/sponsored/house-of-cards/the-ascent/271/.

Auletta, K. 2014. "Why Jill Abramson Was Fired." *New Yorker*, May 14, 2016. www.newyorker.com/business/currency/why-jill-abramson-was-fired.

Auletta, K. 2012. "Citizens Jain." *New Yorker*, October 8, 2012. www.newyorker. com/magazine/2012/10/08/citizens-jain.

Bacon, J. 2016. "Brands Must Adapt to an Ad-Free World, Says Vice Boss Shane Smith." *Marketing Week*, March 23, 2016. www.marketingweek.com/2016/03/23/ brands-must-adapt-to-an-ad-free-world-says-vice-boss-shane-smith/.

Bajak, A. 2016. "How Quartz Is Bringing Storytelling, Interactive Design to Sponsored Content." *Mediashift*, January 11, 2016. http://mediashift.org/2016/01/ how-quartz-is-bringing-storytelling-interactive-design-to-sponsored-content/.

Baker, D. 2016. "Inside The Washington Post's Quest to Fix Ad Tech." *The Content Strategist*, October 6, 2016. https://contently.com/strategist/2016/10/06/ ad-tech-washington-post/.

BBC StoryWorks and Huawei. 2017. "Against All Odds." *BBC Online*. www.bbc. com/storyworks/future/specials/against-all-odds/.

BBC StoryWorks and Skoda. 2016. "The Mind Behind." *BBC Online*. www.bbc. com/storyworks/culture/the-mind-behind/index.

BBC World and Quebec Travel. 2015. "Boundless Adventures." *BBC World Online*. www.bbc.com/travel/bespoke/specials/road-trips-through-quebec/index.html.

Bilton, R. 2016. "The Guardian Is Now Calling Native Ads 'Paid Content'." *Digiday*, January 26, 2016. https://digiday.com/uk/guardian-now-calling-native-ads-paid-content.

Bilton, R. 2014a. "Flush with Cash, Vox Media Seeks a Tech Advantage in Native Ads." *Digiday*, December 2, 2014. https://digiday.com/media/flush-cash-vox-media-seeks-tech-advantage-native-ads.

Bilton, R. 2014b. "Meet the Publishers Who Ask Their Reporters to Write Native Ads – Digiday." *Digiday*, June 5, 2014. https://digiday.com/media/publishers-enlist-reporters-write-native-ad-content/.

Birkner, C. 2016. "Why WSJ's Sponsored Content Features the Economics of Sex and Drugs." *Adweek*, April 7, 2016. www.adweek.com/brand-marketing/ why-wsjs-sponsored-content-features-economics-sex-and-drugs-170666.

Beaujon, A. 2017. "The Washington Post's New Social Media Policy Forbids Disparaging Advertisers." *Washingtonian*, June 27, 2017. www.washingtonian. com/2017/06/27/the-washington-post-social-media-policy.

Bennett, T. 2017. "BuzzFeed CEO Tells Publishers: Remember Who You Are and Play to Your Strengths." *Which-50*, May 29, 2017. https://which-50.com/buzzfeed-ceo-tells-publishers-remember-play-strengths.

BG Brand Lab and Pfizer. 2017. "Dear Scientist." *Boston Globe*. http://sponsored. bostonglobe.com/pfizer/.

BG Brand Lab and Rockland Bank. 2015. "Insights on Building Your Business." *Boston Globe*. http://sponsored.bostonglobe.com/rocklandtrust/.

Bodack, A. 2017. "Turner Ignite Furthers Investment in CNN's Brand Studio Courageous with Promotion of Otto Bell to Chief Creative Officer." *Turner*, September 20, 2017. www.turner.com/pressroom/turner-ignite-furthers-investment-cnn%E2%80%99s-brand-studio-courageous-promotion-otto-bell-chief.

Boland, V. 2017. "Irish Times Appoints New Editor." *Financial Times*, April 5, 2017. www.ft.com/content/b403d960-3b84-387e-beb1-a2f731ebbebc.

Bond, S. 2017. "Time Inc Cuts Dividend and Shakes Up Board as Losses Widen." *Financial Times*, May 10, 2017. www.ft.com/content/ba65f47a-3575-11e7-bce4-9023f8c0fd2e?mhq5j=e1.

Brown, J. 2014. "Leaked Memo Confirms That Globe and Mail Wants Journalists to Write Advertorials." *CANADALAND*, June 10, 2014. www.canadalandshow.com/leaked-memo-confirms-globe-and-mail-wants-journalists-write-advertorials/.

Brownsell, A. 2017. "New York Times SVP Sebastian Tomich: 'It Feels Inevitable That Publishers Will become Agencies'." *MMG*, March 1, 2017. http://mandm global.com/new-york-times-svp-sebastian-tomich-it-feels-inevitable-that-publishers-will-become-agencies.

Brynildsrud, J. I. 2016. "VG'S Movie Partnership Paved Way for Profitable Branded Content Division." *International News Media Association (INMA)*, June 13, 2016. www.inma.org/blogs/ideas/post.cfm/vg-s-movie-partnership-paved-way-for-profitable-branded-content-division.

BuzzFeed and Intel. 2014. "Fifteen Things We Did at School That Future Students Will Never Understand." *BuzzFeed*, August 11, 2014. www.buzzfeed.com/intel/things-we-did-at-school-that-future-students-will-never-u?utm_term=.ykrg4LX 60m#.ctwovYwr6J.

BuzzFeed. n.d. "Advertise with Us." *BuzzFeed*. www.buzzfeed.com/advertise.

Burrell, I. 2017. "The New York Times' Branded Content Studio Is Coming for Ad Agency Business." *The Drum*, July 20, 2017. www.thedrum.com/opinion/2017/07/20/the-new-york-times-branded-content-studio-coming-ad-agency-business.

Burrell, I. 2017. "BuzzFeed's Jonah Peretti: News Publishers Only Have Themselves to Blame for Losing Out to Google and Facebook." *The Drum*, June 29, 2017. www.thedrum.com/opinion/2017/06/29/buzzfeeds-jonah-peretti-news-publishers-only-have-themselves-blame-losing-out.

Davies, J. 2016a. "The BBC Is Launching StoryWorks, an In-House Creative Agency." *The Drum*, June 23, 2016. www.niemanlab.org/reading/the-bbc-is-launching-story works-an-in-house-creative-agency/.

Davies, J. 2016b. "The BBC Is Using Facial Recognition to Measure If Native Ads Work." *Digiday*, January 21, 2016. https://digiday.com/uk/bbc-facial-recognition-native-advertising/.

Davies, J. 2015. "The Financial Times Readies Paid Posts for Advertisers." *Digiday*, September 28, 2015. https://digiday.com/uk/financial-times-readies-paid-posts-advertisers/.

Dvorkin, L. 2016. "Inside Forbes: How Native Ads in Our Magazine Are Inspiring Digital and Video Ideas." *Forbes*, September 13, 2016. www.forbes.com/sites/lewisdvorkin/2016/08/30/inside-forbes-how-native-ads-in-our-magazine-are-inspiring-digital-and-video-ideas/#7d47259531ef.

Elkin, T. 2016. "Politico Focus Aims to Connect Brands with Political Influencers." *MediaPost*, November 30, 2016. www.mediapost.com/publications/article/290004/politico-focus-aims-to-connect-brands-with-politic.html.

*El Pais* and Vodafone. n.d. "El futuro es apasionante." *El Pais*. https://elfuturoesapasionante.elpais.com.

Ember, S. 2017. "New York Times Co. Reports Rising Digital Profit as Print Advertising Falls." *New York Times*, May 3, 2017. www.nytimes.com/2017/05/03/business/new-york-times-co-q1-earnings.html.

Flamm, M. 2017. "Mobile-Focused Startup Quartz Manages to Actually Turn a Profit on Digital Journalism." *Advertising Age*, March 27, 2017. http://adage.com/article/media/mobile-focused-quartz-turns-a-profit-digital-journalism/308440.

FT Square and Auriens. 2017. "Later Life Stories." *Financial Times*. http://laterlifestories.ft.com/the-road-runner/.

FT Squared and VistaJet. 2017. "The Evolution of Private Air Travel." *Financial Times*. http://vistajet.ft.com/the-evolution-of-private-air-travel.

Fuller, Melynda. 2018. "Meredith Corp. Teases Sale of 'Time'." *Mediapost*, March 13, 2018. https://mediapost.com/publications/article/315905/meredith-corp-teases-sale-of-time.html.

Goefron, M. 2015. "BuzzFeed's Editorial Fumble Doesn't Have to Be a Buzzkill for Native Advertising." *Advertising Age*, May 7, 2015. http://adage.com/article/digitalnext/buzzfeed-s-editorial-fumble-a-buzzkill/298386.

Gray, R. 2017. "*The Wall Street Journal's* Global Retrenchment." *The Atlantic*, February 16, 2017. www.theatlantic.com/politics/archive/2017/02/wall-street-journal-retrenches-around-the-world/516915/.

Griffith, E. 2013. "Do Not Expect The New York Times to Go Native." *Pando*, May 7, 2013. https://pando.com/2013/05/07/do-not-expect-the-new-york-times-to-go-native/.

Grinapol, C. 2017. "The Washington Post Is Creating a New Branded Content Offering with Customizable Post Cards." *Adweek*, February 9, 2017. www.adweek.com/digital/the-washington-post-is-creating-a-new-branded-content-offering-with-customizable-post-cards.

Guardian Labs and Seat. 2016. "Inside the Mind of an Innovator." *The Guardian*, May 24, 2016. www.theguardian.com/inside-seat/ng-interactive/2016/may/24/inside-the-mind-of-an-innovator-audio-interactive.

Guardian Labs and Vulcan. 2016. "Elephant Conservation Campaign with Vulcan." *The Guardian*, January 19, 2017. www.theguardian.com/environment/2017/jan/19/if-you-were-an-elephant-.

Guardian Labs and Cisco. 2015. "The Internet of (Nearly) Everything." *The Guardian*, June 17, 2015. www.theguardian.com/media-network/ng-interactive/2015/jun/17/the-internet-of-nearly-everything.

Hagey, K. 2016. "Vice Media Launches Its Own Cable-TV Channel." *Wall Street Journal*, February 29, 2016. www.wsj.com/articles/vice-media-to-launch-its-own-cable-tv-channel-1456696293.

Hansen, T. 2017a. "Boston Globe Media's Brand Studio Works Like a Mini Newsroom." *Native Advertising Institute*, August 7, 2017. https://nativeadvertisinginstitute.com/blog/boston-globe-medias-brand-studio/.

Hansen, T. 2017b. "We Will Be a Replacement for Agencies Unless They Reinvent Themselves." *Native Advertising Institute*, June 21, 2017. https://nativeadverti singinstitute.com/blog/replacement-agencies.

Hansen, T. 2017c. "Why Setting Up a Content Studio Is Strategic to Italian RCS Mediagroup." *Native Advertising Institute*, May 31, 2017. https://nativeadvertising institute.com/blog/content-studio-strategic.

Hansen, T. 2017d. "How One Media Company became the Russian Leader in Native." *Native Advertising Institute*, February 27, 2017. https://nativeadvertisinginstitute. com/blog/leader-in-native.

Heine, C. 2017. "The New York Times' Native Ad Strategy Is Getting a Boost Thanks to These Tech Acquisitions." *Adweek*, June 20, 2017. www.adweek. com/digital/the-new-york-times-native-ad-strategy-is-getting-a-boost-thanks-to-these-tech-acquisitions/.

Horgan, R. 2017. "Forbes Refines Native Ad Strategy with 'Co-Storytelling' Tools." *Adweek*, April 6, 2017. www.adweek.com/brand-marketing/forbes-lewis-dvorkin-native-advertising.

Huffington Post Partner Studio and Caterpillar Foundation. 2017. "From the Ground Up." *HuffingtonPost*. http://partnerstudio.huffingtonpost.com/caterpillar/light-the-way/?sf53363213=1.

IAB UK. "The Telegraph Sets Out Its Vision for Increased Engagement and Transparency across Digital Media." *IAB UK*, March 10, 2017. https://iabuk.net/news/ the-telegraph-sets-out-its-vision-for-increased-engagement-and-transparency-across-digital.

International News Media Association. 2016. "2016 Winner: Montreal Gazette/ Concordia University." *INMA*, 2016. www.inma.org/practice-detail.cfm?zyear= 2016&id=0859EA8D-BE35-4652-B023FB1B5D154FCA.

Irish Times and Audi. 2017. "An Ice Swimmer's Journey through the Best of Both Worlds." *Irish Times*. www.irishtimes.com/sponsored/audi/an-ice-swimmer-s-journey-through-the-best-of-both-worlds-1.2776976.

Jackson, J. 2015. "Telegraph Criticised by Watchdog for 'Misleading' Michelin Advertorial." *The Guardian*, December 30, 2015. www.theguardian.com/media/ 2015/dec/30/telegraph-criticised-asa-watchdog-michelin-advertorial.

Joseph, S. 2016. "Vice Media's CEO Wants to Build a Native Ad Lab to Fix Mobile Monetisation Conundrum." *The Drum*, June 22, 2016. www.thedrum. com/news/2016/06/22/vice-media-s-ceo-wants-build-native-ad-lab-fix-mobile-monetisation-conundrum.

Kelly, K. J. 2017. "Huffington Post Workers Ratify First-Ever Union Contract." *New York Post*, January 30, 2017. http://nypost.com/2017/01/30/huffington-post-workers-ratify-first-ever-union-contract.

Korhonen, P. 2016. "Helsingin Sanomat Markets Its Data Storytelling Tools for Native Advertising Use." *International News Media Association*, April 27, 2016. www.inma.org/blogs/ideas/post.cfm/helsingin-sanomat-markets-its-data-storytelling-tools-for-native-advertising-use.

Kung, L. 2015. *Innovators in digital news*. IB Tauris.

Laursen, J. and Stone, M. 2016. "Native Advertising Trends 2016: The News Media Industry". *The Native Advertising Institute*. https://nativeadvertisinginstitute.com/ wp-content/uploads/2016/10/TrendReportNewsMedia16.pdf.

Lazauskas, J. and Baker, D. 2016. "OMG: You Won't Believe What BuzzFeed Is Doing to Advertising." *The Content Strategist*, April 21, 2016. https://contently.com/strategist/2016/04/21/omg-wont-believe-buzzfeed-advertising.

Lytvynenko, J. 2015. "Emails: Vice Altered Story to Protect 'Relationship' with Rogers." *CANADALAND*, November 30, 2015. www.canadalandshow.com/emails-vice-altered-story-protect-relationship-rogers.

Maerkl, M. 2015. "World in Motion Partnership with GE Takes Content for a Spin." *GE Reports*, May 18, 2015. www.ge.com/reports/post/119377576230/world-in-motion-partnership-with-quartz-takes-ge/.

MCI. 2004. "The New York Times: Advertorial." *New York Times*. www.nytimes.com/marketing/mci/04.html.

MediaRadar Staff. 2017. "How Publishers Maximize Returns on Native Advertising." *MediaRadar*. https://resources.mediaradar.com/blog/how-publishers-maximize-returns-on-native-advertising.

Meduza Staff. 2015. "Нативная Реклама: Почему Это Круто И Почему Ее Никто Не Умеет Делать." *Meduza: How It Works*, October 29, 2015. https://medium.com/meduza-how-it-works/нативная-реклама-почему-это-круто-и-почему-ее-никто-не-умеет-делать-4ae7e060f549.

Moses, L. 2016. "Slate Now Relies on Native Ads for Nearly 50 Percent of Its Revenue." *Digiday*, July 21, 2016. https://digiday.com/media/slate-now-relies-native-ads-nearly-50-percent-revenue.

Moses, L. 2015. "The Washington Post Takes an Amazon-Inspired Approach to Native Ad Targeting." *Digiday*, April 17, 2015. https://digiday.com/media/washington-post-takes-amazon-inspired-approach-native-ad-targeting.

Moses, L. 2014. "The Washington Post's Native Ads Get Editorial Treatment." *Adweek*, March 3, 2014. www.adweek.com/digital/washington-posts-native-ads-get-editorial-treatment-156048.

Moses, L. 2012. "'Atlantic,' 'Economist,' Duke It Out for Elites." *Adweek*, June 5, 2012. www.adweek.com/digital/atlantic-economist-duke-it-out-elites-140897/.

Mullin, B. 2017. "Vox Media Pitches Signature 'Explainer' Format to Advertisers." *Wall Street Journal*, October 13, 2017. www.wsj.com/articles/vox-media-pitches-signature-explainer-format-to-advertisers-1507892401.

Mullins, L. 2016. "Inside the Politico Break-Up." *Washingtonian*, July 17, 2016. www.washingtonian.com/2016/07/17/politico-breakup-vandehei-allbritton-allen.

Murrell, C. 2016. "The Guardian's Costly Gap between Traffic and Profits." *The Conversation*, February 29, 2016. http://theconversation.com/the-guardians-costly-gap-between-traffic-and-profits-55388.

Notting, T. 2016. "Burda Forward Baut Native Advertising Aus." *W&V*, March 29, 2016. www.wuv.de/digital/burda_forward_baut_native_advertising_aus.

O'Berne, R. 2014. "J-Source's Top 10 Journalism Stories of 2014." *J-Source*, December 19, 2014. www.j-source.ca/article/j-source's-top-10-journalism-stories-2014.

Oborne, P. 2015. "Why I Have Resigned from the Telegraph." *openDemocracy*, February 17, 2015. www.opendemocracy.net/ourkingdom/peter-oborne/why-i-have-resigned-from-telegraph.

Peretti, J. 2015. "Why BuzzFeed Does News." *BuzzFeed*, June 18, 2015. www.buzzfeed.com/jonah/why-buzzfeed-does-news?utm_term=.ropV1RJ2o#.oiwD64Mwn.

Politico Focus and J. P. Morgan Chase. 2017. "A Model of Recovery for America's Cities." *Politico*, May 18, 2017. www.politico.com/sponsor-content/2017/05/model-of-recovery-for-americas-cities?sr_source=lift_amplify&cid=20175hp.

Politico Focus and American Chemistry Council. 2015. "From the Salt of the Earth." *Politico*. www.politico.com/sponsor-content/2015/06/element-of-suprise/.

Quartz Bulletins and Siemens. 2015. "How Data Is Generating Green Lights to Keep You Moving on the Road." *Quartz*. https://qz.com/391157/how-data-is-generating-green-lights-to-keep-you-moving-on-the-road/.

Raudenbush, R. 2015. "How Politico Crafts Branded Content with a Political Agenda." *Digiday*, July 24, 2015. https://digiday.com/media/politico-brand-content.

RCS. 2017. "RCS Pubblicità per la Rinascente." *RCS Mediagroup*, May 24, 2017. www.rcsmediagroup.it/comunicati/comunicato-stampa-rcs-pubblicita-per-la-rinascente.

RCS. 2015. "Hyundai e RCS insieme per la campagna 'CHANGE IS GOOD'." *RCS Mediagroup*, October 22, 2015. www.rcsmediagroup.it/comunicati/hyundai-e-rcs-insieme-per-la-campagna-change-is-good/.

Reunanen, E. 2017. "Finland." *Reuters Digital News Report*. www.digitalnews report.org/survey/2016/finland-2016/.

Robischon, N. 2016. "How Buzzfeed's Jonah Perretti is Building a 100-Year Media Company." Fast Company, February 2, 2016. www.fastcompany.com/3056057/how-buzzfeeds-jonah-peretti-is-building-a-100-year-media-company.

Rodriguez, A. 2016. "How a Single Deal with a Decidedly Unhip Tech Company Built the Vice Media Behemoth." *Quartz*, September 8, 2016. http://qz.com/776628/shane-smith-how-a-single-native-advertising-deal-with-intel-intc-built-the-vice-media-behemoth.

Sainath, P. 2010. "Paid News Undermining Democracy: Press Council Report." *The Hindu*, April 21, 2010. www.thehindu.com/opinion/columns/sainath/Paid-news-undermining-democracy-Press-Council-report/article16371596.ece.

Schibsted Brand Studio. 2016. "A Perfect Match." *Schibsted Future Report*. https://futurereport.schibsted.com/a-perfect-match/.

Schibsted Media Group. 2015. "Editorial Report: Journalism in New Ways." Schibsted 2015 Annual Report. www.schibsted.com/en/Annual-Report-2015/Sustainability/People-and-society/.

Schibsted Media Group. 2016. "Annual Report." *Schibsted Media Group*. http://hugin.info/131/R/2096898/793519.pdf.

Sebastian, M. 2015. "Native Ads Were 'Inside' 10% of Digital at The New York Times Last Year." *Advertising Age*, February 3, 2015. http://adage.com/article/media/york-times-sold-18-2- million-worth-native-ads/296966.

Sebastian, M. 2013. "Associated Press Is the Latest News Organization to Try Sponsored Content." *Advertising Age*, October 18, 2013. http://adage.com/article/media/press- sponsored-content/244817.

SlateCustom and Siemens. 2016. "Ingenious Cities." *Slate*, April, 2016. www.slate.com/articles/technology/siemens/2016/05/ingenious_cities.html.

SlateCustom and Wells Fargo. 2014a. "Does Viral Philanthropy Really Work?" *Slate*, November 12, 2014. www.slate.com/articles/life/wells_fargo_2/2014/11/does_viral_philanthropy_really_work.html.

SlateCustom and Wells Fargo. 2014b. "Beatboxing Transforms Education at Lavelle School for the Blind." *Slate*, October 10, 2014. www.slate.com/articles/life/wells_fargo/2014/10/beatboxing_transforms_education_at_lavelle_school_for_the_blind.html.

Sloane, G. 2016. "Inside The Washington Post's Internal Agency and Its Growing Ambitions." *Digiday*, May 16, 2016. https://digiday.com/media/inside-washington-posts-million-dollar-branded-content-team.

Sonderman, J. and Tran, M. 2013. "Understanding the Rise of Sponsored Content." *American Press Institute*, November 13, 2013. www.americanpressinstitute.org/publications/reports/white-papers/understanding-rise-sponsored-content/.

Southern, L. 2016a. "How the Atlantic's Content-Marketing Division Is Expanding Internationally." *Digiday*, June 24, 2016. https://digiday.com/uk/atlantics-branded-content-division-driving-international-expansion.

Southern, L. 2016b. "With Print's Future in Peril, El Pais Hones Its Online Editorial Strategy." *Digiday*, May 12, 2016. https://digiday.com/uk/prints-future-peril-el-pais-looks-editorial-curation-online/.

Stack, L. 2015. "BuzzFeed Says Posts Were Deleted Because of Advertising Pressure." *New York Times*, April 19, 2015. www.nytimes.com/2015/04/20/business/media/buzzfeed-says-posts-were-deleted-because-of-advertising-pressure.html?_r=0.

Standage, T. 2016. "Economist Digital Strategy Chief: We Expect Display Advertising to Have Disappeared by 2025." *Press Gazette*, December 20, 2016. www.pressgazette.co.uk/economist-digital-strategy-chief-we-expect-display-advertising-to-have-disappeared-by-2025/.

Sterne, P. 2014. "Former Vice Media Editor Says Company Killed Stories over 'Brand Partner' Concerns." *Politico*, October 2, 2014. www.politico.com/media/story/2014/10/former-vice-media-editor-says-company-killed-stories-over-brand-partner-concerns-002932.

Stipp, N. and GNM Press Office. 2012. "The Guardian Is Now the World's Third Most Read Newspaper Website." *The Guardian*, July 26, 2012. www.theguardian.com/gnm-press-office/8.

Sternberg, J. 2012. "The Economist's Content Marketing Bid." *Digiday*, November 20, 2012. https://digiday.com/media/the-economist-content-marketing-approach/.

StoryPlus and Ireland's Ancient East. 2017. "Behind the Doors of Big Houses in Ireland's Ancient East." *Independent Online*, June 1, 2017. www.independent.ie/editorial/StoryPlus/behind-the-doors-of-big-houses-in-relands-ancient-east/.

StoryPlus and MiniCooper. 2017. "Behind Every Mini . . ." *Independent Online*, March 7, 2017. www.independent.ie/editorial/StoryPlus/behind-every-mini/.

Sullivan, M. 2017. "Perspective | The Atlantic Is 'Most Vital When America Is Most Fractured.' Good Thing It Soars Today." *Washington Post*, July 23, 2017. www.washingtonpost.com/lifestyle/style/the-atlantic-is-most-vital-when-america-is-fractured-good-thing-it-soars-today/2017/07/21/11ce818e-6d46-11e7-96ab-5f38140b38cc_story.html.

Swaine, J. 2014. "Vice's Shane Smith: 'Young People Are Angry and Leaving TV in Droves'." *The Guardian*, March 2, 2014. www.theguardian.com/media/2014/mar/02/vice-media-shane-smith-north-korea.

Sweney, M. 2012. "BBC World Service to Run Ads on Some Websites and Radio Stations." *The Guardian*, January 5, 2012. www.theguardian.com/media/2012/jan/05/bbc-world-service-ads.

Sweney, M. 2014. GNM Launches Branded Content Division Guardian Labs. *The Guardian*, February 13, 2914. www.theguardian.com/media/2014/feb/13/guardian-labs-branded-content.

Takahashi, D. 2015. "How 98-Year-Old Forbes Media Generates 70% of Its Revenues from Digital." *VentureBeat*, July 13, 2015. https://venturebeat.com/2015/07/13/how-98-year-old-forbes-media-generates-70-of-its-revenues-from-digital.

Taube, A. 2015. "The One Thing That Makes Quartz Stand Out from Its Competition." *NATIVE*, March 2, 2015. http://nativeadvertising.com/one-thing-that-makes-quartz-stand-out-from-its-competition.

T Brand Studio. 2017. "Stories That Influence the Influential." *T Brand Studio*. www.tbrandstudio.com.

T Brand Studio and MilkPep. 2017. "A Fresh Look." *New York Times*. https://paidpost.nytimes.com/milkpep/a-fresh-look.html.

T Brand Studio and Sothebys. 2017. "The Art of Living with and within Art." *New York Times*. https://paidpost.nytimes.com/sothebys/the-art-of-living-with-and-within-art.html.

T Brand Studio and Tropicana. 2017. "The Perfect Sip." *New York Times*. https://paidpost.nytimes.com/tropicana/the-perfect-sip.html.

T Brand Studio and GE. 2016. "How Nature Is Inspiring Our Industrial Future." *New York Times*. https://paidpost.nytimes.com/ge/how-nature-is-inspiring-our-industrial-future.html.

T Brand Studio and Cole Haan. 2015. "Grit and Grace." *New York Times*. https://paidpost.nytimes.com/cole-haan/grit-and-grace.html.

T Brand Studio and Netflix. 2014. "Women Inmates: Why the Male Model Doesn't Work." *New York Times*. https://paidpost.nytimes.com/netflix/women-inmates-separate-but-not-equal.html.

Teicher, J. 2016. "How The New York Times Took Native Advertising Global." *The Content Strategist*, November 16, 2016. https://contently.com/strategist/2016/11/16/new-york-times-native-advertising.

Telegraph and Flanders Tourism. 2012. "Sights and Attractions along the Flanders Coast." *The Telegraph*, October 25, 2012. www.telegraph.co.uk/sponsored/travel/flanders-coast/9625335/flanders-coast-attractions-sights.html.

Times of India. 2003. "Medianet: Innovative Content, Integrated Offering." *Times of India*, March 4, 2003. http://timesofindia.indiatimes.com/india/Medianet-Innovative-content-integrated-offering/articleshow/39286961.cms.

Tomkiw, L. 2015. "With Aggregation and Translation, Russia's Free-Press-in-Exile Site Meduza Is Reaching English Readers." *NiemanLab*, February 6, 2015. www.niemanlab.org/2015/02/with-aggregation-and-translation-russias-free-press-in-exile-site-meduza-is-reaching-english-readers.

Trotter, J. K. 2015. "BuzzFeed Deletes Post Critical of Dove, A BuzzFeed Advertiser." *Gawker*, April 9, 2015. http://tktk.gawker.com/buzzfeed-deletes-post-critical-of-dove-a-buzzfeed-adve-1696852834.

Uberti, D. 2016. "What A Major Leadership Change Means For Politico's Global Ambitions." *Columbia Journalism Review*. www.cjr.org/analysis/politico.php.

Van Zuylen-Wood, S. 2017. "Can Linda Henry Save the Boston Globe?" *Boston Magazine*, May 21, 2017. www.bostonmagazine.com/news/2017/05/21/linda-pizzuti-henry-boston-globe/.

Verne and Ecoalf. 2015. "¿Apago el aire acondicionado o lo dejo encendido? Ahorrar en casa y en la oficina." *El País*. https://verne.elpais.com/verne/2017/06/09/articulo/1497016528_788937.html.

Vice and Smirnoff. 2017. "Let's Double the Women Headliners in Electronic Music." *Vice*, March 9, 2017. https://partners.vice.com/smirnoff/equalizingmusicarticle/news/double-the-women-headliners/.

Vice and Western Union. 2017. "New Life, New Land." *Vice*. https://partners.vice.com/western-union/newlifenewland/.

Vice and Western Union. 2016. "Through the Lens of a Refugee." *Vice*. https://partners.vice.com/western-union/newlifenewland/news/b0bc1607308e162aac06d2288e2bb13b/.

Willens, M. 2016. "From Native Ads to Niche Sites: How Time Inc. Changed under Joe Ripp." *Digiday*, September 13, 2016. https://digiday.com/media/native-ads-niche-sites-time-inc-changed-joe-ripp/.

Williams, C. 2017. "Guardian Claims Progress on Heavy Losses as It Holds Talks on Manchester Move." *The Telegraph*, April 27, 2017. www.telegraph.co.uk/business/2017/04/27/guardian-claims-progress-heavy-losses-holds-talks-manchester.

Wiser, M. "The Worst Examples of Native Advertising." *Mobile Advertising Watch*, October 24, 2013. mobileadvertisingwatch.com/worst-examples-native-advertising-556.

WP Brand Studio and Paramount. 2017. "An Inconvenient Sequel: Truth to Power." *Washington Post*. www.washingtonpost.com/sf/brand-connect/paramount/truth-to-power-the-inconvenient-voices-taking-on-climate-change/.

WP Brand Studio and Philips. 2017. "Transforming Healthcare to a Value-Based Payment System." *Washington Post*. www.washingtonpost.com/sf/brand-connect/philips/transforming-healthcare/.

WP Brand Studio and Syfy. 2016. "Shadow Mission." *Washington Post*. www.washingtonpost.com/sf/brand-connect/syfy/shadow-mission/?tid=a_mcntx.

WP Brand Studio and Sub Zero. n.d. "Solving the Problem of Food Waste." *Washington Post*. www.washingtonpost.com/sf/brand-connect/sub-zero/solving-the-problem-of-food-waste/.

WSJ Custom Studios and PWC. 2017. "Broader Perspectives: A Cybersecurity and Privacy Hub." *Wall Street Journal*. http://sponsoredcontent.wsj.com/pwc/broader-perspectives/.

WSJ Custom Studios and Starz. 2016. "The Business of the Heart." *Wall Street Journal*. http://partners.wsj.com/starz/the-girlfriend-experience/.

WSJ Custom Studios and Netflix. 2015. "Cocainenomics." *Wall Street Journal*. www.wsj.com/ad/cocainenomics.

# 3    Native on the issues

## Native advertising and issue-based messaging from corporations and nonprofits

In the summer of 2017, Hyatt Regency Hotels ran a native advertising campaign in *The Atlantic* focused on the topic of race relations. Titled "Speaking of Hope," the ad led with an anecdote in which US civil rights activist Xernona Clayton described how she and others faced discrimination while organizing the Southern Christian leadership Conference's tenth anniversary convention in Atlanta. While attempting to book a hotel, they were told by the hotel's manager, "we don't like you coming here." Clayton explains that she then turned to the Hyatt Regency:

> "The timing was right for the Hyatt Regency Atlanta, because we were looking for a friendly place," said Clayton. "Everybody was welcome. And then more places like that started to pop up. That's when the city finally started to change." Over the past 50 years, she added, the hotel has held true to the vision: It has always been a place where all are welcome, where groups consistently come together; it is the hotel of hope.
> (Atlantic Re:Think and Hyatt 2017)

The branding of the Regency as the "hotel of hope" carries through the campaign, which continues with a series of anecdotes about Clayton's efforts to overcome racial bigotry from the 1940s to the present, as well as additional videos in which Clayton discusses racism with a young performer named Tarronia "Tank" Bell. The centerpiece of the ad is a video of "Tank" performing a spoken-word piece titled "Come Together," which links the civil rights movement to more recent collective action for social justice. The takeaway from video and overall campaign is that the Regency is a welcoming place for all, but also a fellow-traveler in the struggle for racial equality in the US.

In aligning its brand with a social message, Hyatt is hardly breaking new ground; the roots of such socially-minded advertising can be traced back to 1960s campaigns including those for Volkswagen and Coca-Cola. But the format – that of an online magazine news feature, albeit one labeled as an advertisement – *is* new. Hyatt's campaign is part of a wave of native advertising that focuses on social or political issues, either as a to promote a product or to promote a concept or ideology. Sometimes the messages in such campaigns (like Hyatt's) are upbeat and uncontroversial. At other times, however, issue-based native advertising is used to recuperate tarnished corporate images, intervene in policy debates, and even to hype political candidates. In other words, these ads muster the persuasive tactics of conventional advertising in order to promote not just consumption, but real-world change, sometimes blurring the lines between editorial coverage of social issues and promoted content serving corporate interests.

As US and European regulators attempt to refine standards for native advertising, issue-based advertising seems to be slipping between the cracks: regulators have been focusing largely on protecting consumers from misleading messages about brands, while the potential effects of the persuasive power of issue ads that borrow credibility from news media has drawn far less scrutiny. This chapter argues that these ads can provide disproportionate amplification of corporate speech, lend credibility to one-sided arguments, and in some cases overpower the agenda-setting function of the press, focusing attention on issues and causes that serve corporate interests or advance a nonprofit's agenda.

In this chapter, I survey a range of issue-based native advertising, including ads from the energy industry, from the health care sector, from corporations looking to associate themselves with causes, and from nonprofits and political candidates. I show that such ads build on advertising and public relations practices that predate native advertising, sometimes by more than a century. By looking at the representational strategies of these ads and analysing their messaging, I show how these practices have been modified in ways that potentially change how news audiences perceive both the advertising and the issues it addresses. I conclude by exploring the particular dangers such advertising poses to civic dialogue, building on my earlier discussion of legal and ethical concerns about native advertising.

## The roots of issue-based native: institutional advertising, paid op-eds, and corporate sponsorships

In Chapter 1, I noted that some advertising scholars see native advertising as just another iteration in the broader category of "advertorials." Issue-based native advertising has been similarly described as the latest form of what used to be called "institutional advertising," campaigns run by corporations or nonprofits that attempt to influence public opinion or bolster the image of the advertiser. Scholarly study of institutional advertising has not been as extensive as study of brand advertising. A series of studies beginning in the 1970s described the trend optimistically, seeing it as an effective avenue of social change (Zeigler 1970; Kotler and Zaltman 1971). Later research, however, was more critical. As early as 1978, management scholar Prakash Sethi questioned whether the increased visibility of commercial speech attempting to influence public opinion might have long-term social consequences (Sethi 1978). In 1980, political scientist Robert Meadow expressed alarm about the rise in institutional "advocacy" advertising, noting that such ads provided "a forum for direct access to voters through grassroots lobbying which supplements the more traditional forms of corporate public relations and political participation." Further studies raised concerns about the possibility that readers would confuse institutional ads with editorial content (Kim, Pasadeos and Barban 2001) and noted that effectiveness of such advertising was difficult to measure (Cooper and Nownes 2004; Schuman, Hathcote and West 1991).

In the United States, the emergence of institutional advertising can be traced be the early 1900s, when AT&T relied on the practice as a means of persuading a disenchanted public that it should remain an independent company with limited government oversight (Marchand 1987). The strategy was later used by railroads, steel companies, and meat packers to similarly argue against government interference; by businesses looking to recoup reputations during the Great Depression; and by the US Advertising Council to promote free markets at the end of the Second World War. In Europe, institutional advertising was slower to develop (Shell's iconic British campaigns can be seen as early examples), but by the 1970s both European and international campaigns began to emerge, as corporations increasingly believed they had "the right and the obligation to participate in public debate on controversial issues of public policy" (Waltzer 1988, 55). Still, a tighter regulatory environment around political advertising in many countries outside the US has meant that for the most part, the practice of institutional advertising has been more explicitly political in the US than elsewhere.

Beyond institutional advertising, corporations and nonprofits also have a long history of courting public favor through sponsorship of radio and television programming. As with institutional advertising, corporate sponsorship of broadcasting has been less common in Europe. In some countries (such as Britain) such sponsorship has been prohibited in the public broadcasting sector, while in others (including Germany and France) corporate sponsorship was allowed only after the 1960s (EPRA 2006). In the US, scholars have chronicled how sponsorship was used to great advantage by tobacco, alcohol, and energy industries (Barnouw 1978; Haley 1996; Meenaghan 2001), with sponsors serving as "remote and unseen, but omnipresent" figures who both confer authority on the televised proceedings and draw legitimacy from their sponsorships (Barnouw ibid, 1). Corporate sponsorship has also been linked to corporate censorship of US public broadcasting. During the 1970s and 1980s the oil industry sponsored more than 70 percent of US prime-time public television, including the much-lauded *Masterpiece Theatre*. During this period, documentaries critical of mining or drilling practices were blocked by stations that accepted such sponsorships (Starr 2001, 47).

While broadcast sponsorship has been around for nearly a century, the adoption of corporate sponsorship outside of the broadcast arena became widespread only towards the turn of the millennium (Meenaghan 2001). Corporate sponsorship of print media is a relatively new phenomenon, made possible by the rise of digital media and the rise of in-house content studios at news outlets searching for creative ways to fund content. Though corporate sponsorship is not technically "advertising" in the sense of a creative campaign distributed to a target audience, native advertising has blurred the distinction between advertising and sponsorship in the print and digital space. As discussed in Chapter 1, native advertising is often referred to as "sponsored content," and that descriptive term is often taken in the broadest sense by native advertising studios at news outlets. While much "sponsored content" is advertising produced by these content studios, in some cases "sponsorship" refers to the underwriting of editorially produced articles, article series, or entire content sections by the corporation in question. Almost always, such sponsored articles or sections are related to issues or causes, even if the advertiser in question sells products to consumers. And, as we will discuss, these sponsorships are usually meant to advance an ideological agenda, boost a flagging reputation, or align the corporation with a particular issue. Consequently, in this chapter, I consider such sponsorships alongside conventional native advertising.

## Big oil and soft power: from paid op-eds to native ads

Over the course of the 20th century, the energy industry ranked among the world's most prolific, and most controversial, institutional advertisers. During the same period in which the energy industry engaged in widespread corporate sponsorship of US public broadcasting, it also helped to launch a second wave of advocacy advertising, this time focusing not only on reputation control, but also on shaping elite discourse. As Brown and Waltzer explain (2005), such energy advertisements were "sponsored to reach the eyes and ears of target publics, and . . . to influence their sociopolitical views and behaviors." The target audiences in question included both the general public, reached through publication in outlets such as *Time* magazine, and political elites, reached via outlets such as *The New York Times*.

After *The New York Times* began the practice of running paid op-eds in the lower right quadrant of the editorial page in 1970, Mobil purchased space on the editorial page of the Thursday issue of the *Times* for three decades, reducing its ad buy to every other Thursday after merging with Exxon in 1999.

Mobil's op-eds were largely text-based but occasionally included simple graphs or illustrative pull quotes. They celebrated the company's achievements, suggested that cars and highways served the country better than public transportation, pushed back against criticism of the energy industry during the 1970s energy crisis, and, starting in the 1990s, laid the foundation for skepticism around climate change. Notable among the latter were a series of op-eds that ran prior to the Kyoto Summit in 1997, arguing that industry self-regulation was superior to the regulatory solutions proposed in the Kyoto Treaty. Other op-eds ranged even further afield, weighing in on topics such as free markets, trade competitiveness, tort reform, and the need for a looser regulatory climate (ExxonMobil 2000).

Scrutinizing the intention and effects of such ads, researchers and legal experts have suggested that the persistent, congenial, and persuasive op-eds authored by Mobil and Exxon Mobil were a deliberate attempt to mislead the public by an industry which – like the tobacco industry – had long conducted internal research suggesting the opposite of what their advertisements claimed. In 2016, New York State District Attorney Erik Schneiderman began a fraud investigation based on these advertising practices, and though the case is still pending, both academic (Supran and Oreskes 2017) and journalistic (Funk 2016) investigations have unearthed compelling evidence that these ads misled the public, deliberately borrowing the credibility of the news organizations that they advertised in to give their claims authority (Smith et al. 2014).

Given this history, it is noteworthy that the energy industry has been an enthusiastic client of the new content studios at print and online media outlets. Like earlier energy op-eds, native advertising produced on behalf of the energy industry focuses on giving the industry a "place at the table" in conversations about energy policy and energy use. Unlike these earlier advertisements, however, the approach is usually far subtler. Rather than challenging climate science, these campaigns emphasize the idea that the energy industry is the primary engine of growth and innovation and that research advances have made the industry safer and more efficient.

This approach is evident in early native advertising produced for Shell by the *New York Times* and the *Washington Post*, two outlets that counted the oil company among their earliest native clients. A few examples show the range of approaches. In 2014, a Shell advertisement in the *Post* focused on reducing the environmental impact of driving (T Brand Studio and Shell

2014). In 2014, the *Times* ran a campaign for Shell called "Cities Energized," featuring a video in which Shell executive Jeremy Bentham described cooperation between governments and corporations in the effort to build sustainable cities (T Brand Studio and Shell 2014). And in 2015, another *Times* campaign for Shell titled "Powering Human Progress" chronicled Shell's efforts in clean energy research such as wind and solar (T Brand Studio and Shell 2015).

Shell's efforts to rebrand itself as a company with an environmental mission – a strategy often labeled "greenwashing" (Laufer 2003) – has been a common practice in recent energy industry advertising, including native advertising. In 2017, American Fuel and Petrochemical Manufacturers, an industry lobby association, created a native campaign with WP Brand Studio titled "Oil Refiners and Petrochemical Producers Are Crucial in the Drive to Save Energy": this ad detailed how a boom in shale oil and gas production has led to more raw material to produce plastic parts for lighter, more energy-efficient vehicles (WP Brand Studio and American Fuel Petrochemical Manufacturers 2017). Similarly, a 2016 T Brand Studio campaign for Chevron identified natural gas as a "cleaner-burning fossil fuel," and a 2017 T Brand Studio ad for GE focused on "bio-inspiration" or research that studies biological systems to improve energy efficiency (T Brand Studio and Chevron 2016).

These ads are a far cry from Mobil's earlier efforts to deny the reality of climate change; instead, they acknowledge the need for shifts in how energy is produced and consumed, but also suggest the energy industry itself is best positioned to determine the extent and direction of such shifts. An exemplary campaign in this regard was a series produced by T Brand Studio for Statoil titled "A Different Look at Energy." The campaign focused on four initiatives in the US and Europe in which Statoil had used innovative techniques to promote efficiency and sustainability, including improved water conservation in shale oil production, the reduction of drilling time in well creation, and the adaptation of techniques from the aerospace industry in energy production. In a video documenting the relationship between oil industry research and the aerospace industry, a female scientist wonders, "how do we keep the planet healthy enough to sustain us?" and compares her research to ballet, a dance in the laboratory intended to "make life better" (T Brand Studio and Statoil 2017). Aside from aestheticizing the process of oil industry research, the campaign positions Statoil as a global healer; the images of space in the video suggest that Statoil has a unique, holistic perspective on sustainability.

Such "green" representations have been the dominant strategy used in the energy industry to promote a better corporate image, but not the only strategy. Another strain of advertising has focused on damage control in the wake of industry accidents and subsequent criticism. This practice, like "greenwashing" tactics, predates native advertising. In the 1970s, when institutional advertising re-emerged in force, PR handbooks explicitly encouraged corporations and lobby groups to mount advertorial campaigns as a counter offensive against critics (Brown and Waltzer 2005). Though research has suggested such advertising is not generally effective at restoring trust (Bodkin, Amato and Amato 2015), it remains a common means of damage control. For example, in the 2017 campaign "Forewarned is Forewarned," produced by WP Brand Studio and published in both the *Atlantic* and *The Washington Post*, British Petroleum (BP) identified technologies created in the wake of the Deepwater Horizon spill that allowed the oil and gas industry "to identify risks before they become crises." A later advertisement in *Politico*, "360 Degrees of Safety," focused on one such technological innovation – the use of a VR simulation to train offshore drilling crews how to respond to a disaster.

This use of native advertising as a counter-offensive strategy is not, of course, limited to the energy industry. In fact, the oft-derided 2013 Scientology campaign in the *Atlantic* discussed in Chapter 1 is an example of this practice: Scientology leader David Miscavige touted the religious group's "milestone year" and the opening of dozens of new churches in an article timed to blunt the effect of a critical book on Scientology scheduled for publication the following week (Voorhees 2013). Drawing from the same playbook, Nestle, after being sharply criticized in 2016 and 2017 for its attempts to hoard clean water in wells near the contaminated Flint, Michigan water system (Glenzian 2017), partnered with T Brand Studio on a native series centered on water management. Titled "Working Together for Water," the campaign described Nestle's "global stewardship" of water sources (T Brand Studio and Nestle 2017), recasting the company in a custodial, rather than hoarding, role. And, when evidence began to mount that laptops in the university classroom distracted students and led to poor information retention (May 2017), *BBC* partnered with Microsoft on a native campaign titled "Laptop Learning" focusing on the benefits of classroom laptop use (BBC StoryWorks and Microsoft 2016).

Native advertisements such as these are classic examples of spin updated for the 21st century. They are perhaps closer to traditional public relations than advertising, except that instead of being "earned" media, they are paid campaigns cloaked in a format that aligns stylistically with the editorial content of their partner publication. Their positive messages are intended to balance out media criticism of their advertisers – criticism that, in some cases, has appeared in the same publications as the advertisements themselves (as one example, *The New York Times* published articles critical of Nestle's water practices around the same time that "Working Together for

Water" was published). Given that the intent of a native ad is to be taken as seriously as editorial content, potential conflicts between the rosy view of native advertising and critical reporting on the activities of corporations create a sense of dissonance within a publication, leaving a reader unsure where the reality might lie.

An example of this dissonance occurred in *Politico* in in the immediate aftermath of the Deepwater Horizon Spill, when the outlet published an article – written by a BP communications spokesperson – that argued that the spill had only a minimal effect on the Gulf region. Insisting "advocacy groups cherry-pick(ed) evidence and blame(d) BP for any and all environmental problems afflicting the Gulf," the piece echoed the dismissive language of early Exxon Mobile op-eds used to disparage climate science. However, this PR-department-authored article was *not* a paid op-ed – and initially not even labeled as an opinion piece. *Politico* relabelled it as an opinion piece only after the article drew the attention of *Washington Post* media critic Erik Wemple in the *Washington Post*, who dubbed the BP article "free native advertising" for BP and speculated that *Politico* published the piece in return for BP's frequent sponsorship of *Politico*'s "Playbook" section. Wemple noted that "BP frequently sponsored Mike Allen's phenomenal 'Playbook' and often drew favorable free mentions from Allen within . . . [Allen's] daily newsletter" (Wemple 2014).

Not satisfied by *Politico*'s decision to relabel the content, Wemple asked *Politico* "whether another piece written solely from the point of view of a single corporation had been in that 'opinion' content basket . . . [and] received no on-the-record response."

The *Politico* article was not the first time BP had been accused of slanting the truth – the companies' aggressive attempts at greenwashing, including the "Beyond Petroleum" campaign created by Oglivy and Mather in 2000, had engendered widespread criticism for its exaggeration of BP's investments in alternative energy (Solman 2008; Murphy 2002). But the fact that *Politico* gave the company a platform to do so for free is discomfiting, and suggests that the companies' financial clout may have pushed *Politico*, at least, to lend its publication's credibility and authority to BP in a manner that blurred the lines between advertising and editorial.

In Chapter 1, I discussed the potential for the kind of cronyism – or at least *perception* of cronyism – that is suggested by the BP article in *Politico*. Whatever one concludes about the relationship between *Politico* and BP, there is increasing evidence that in the weakened US news market, publicists and corporate PR departments have begun to press for, and offer money for, editorial coverage that aligns with their own mandates (Christian 2018). The coziness embodied in native advertising "partnerships," especially those which extend to the sponsorship of editorial content, make this type of payola arrangement seem less outrageous than it might have a few years ago.[1]

## Native advertising and health care

Like the energy industry, the health care industry is a major source of revenue for native content studios at news outlets. And like energy native advertising, health care native campaigns are the latest innovation in an industry with an often controversial advertising legacy, beginning with investigations into claims about "patent medicines" in the early 1900s (Donohue 2006). Though health advertising is heavily regulated in both the US and Europe, scholars have remained concerned about its effects on both health care policy (West, Heith and Goodwin 1996) and consumer behaviour, establishing ties between emergence of direct-to-consumer (DTC) pharmaceutical advertising and a rise in healthcare costs (Frosch et al. 2007).

Over the past decade, the emergence of a series of consumer-facing and physician-facing portals such as Medscape, WebMD, and Everyday Health changed the market for health care advertising, attracting a large share of both native and programmatic advertising as well as content sponsorships from the drug companies. In some cases, the advertising practices of these digital portals have drawn scrutiny: for example, a 2010 quiz authored by Eli Lilly and posted to the health portal WebMD suggested to everyone who completed the quiz that they were at risk for depression and should consider consulting a doctor (Teicher 2017). Health care native campaigns at news outlets have generally been more fastidious, steering away from the overt marketing of drugs. A sampling of campaigns for hospitals, insurance companies, health nonprofits, and pharmaceutical companies demonstrate a range of approaches from commissioned research to advance a policy position, to emotional appeals meant to draw attention and funding to medical issues.

The research-based approach is exemplified by *The Economist's* native advertising division Intelligence Unit, which partnered with insurance company Cigna on a campaign about opioids featuring a downloadable whitepaper on US approaches to opioid addiction (Economist Intelligence Unit and Cigna 2017), and with Gilead – a company that has been controversial for high drug pricing – on a global study about access to healthcare (Economist and Gilead 2017). That study, which surveyed health care systems in 60 countries, called for policy work to establish consistent health care across national markets (and presumably, consistent demand for Gilead's products).

*The Economist*'s campaigns are among the few that have emerged from European news outlets; many more examples can be found in the US, where the looser regulatory environment around advertising has combined with a commercial health care system in crisis to create a strong market for native health care advertising. Responding to the sense of crisis, some of these health care campaigns resemble energy industry advertising in the manner in which they persuade the reader that the industry is best positioned to assess regulatory frameworks and suggest appropriate policy responses. Examples include a *Politico* advertisement for Pfizer titled "Harnessing Innovation to Create Health Care Policies That Matter," which argues for regulatory policies friendly to health care innovation (Politico and Pfizer 2017); an Athena Health campaign for the *Atlantic* titled "A Mission To Heal" that focused on praising the Accountable Care organizations established under the Affordable Care Act (Atlantic Re:Think and Athena 2017); and another *Politico* campaign for the American Cancer Society, which used the idea of an online candlelight vigil to lobby for more government spending on cancer in response to research cutbacks (Politico and American Cancer Society 2015).

Additionally, the adversarial climate around health care delivery has led a number of advertisers to use dramatic patient stories in native campaigns in order to humanize health care corporations and position them as caring partners instead of profit-centered companies. For example, Optum, a US company specializing in managing chronic illness, partnered with Bloomberg Media on a campaign called "Day Zero," a short film about a hepatitis patient who needs a second liver transplant. The patient, an elderly, gay flight attendant, develops a close relationship with the Optum care coordinator who remotely organizes his transplant: at the end of the film, the two finally meet and share a weepy embrace (Bloomberg and Optum 2017). In a similar vein, Pfizer and *The Boston Globe* created a campaign called "Dear Scientist," in which families affected by diseases such as Parkinson's write a letter to a Pfizer scientist about how their lives have been affected by the disease. A series of videos show the scientists who read each letter meeting the families in an emotional exchange about their suffering and hope for a cure (BG Brand Lab and Pfizer 2017).

Aside from being an attempt to humanize pharmaceutical research, the Pfizer ad is an example of how drug companies are marketing their wares indirectly, using the associative logic of native advertising as a means to persuade without creating an actual DTC advertisement. There are further examples of this strategy in both the US and in Europe, where DTC health advertising is prohibited (Leonardo et al. 2007). In 2016, Eli Lilly partnered with *Politico* on a campaign that lobbied for policy changes that would have made it easier for them to test and then market their new Alzheimer's drug, solanezumab; unfortunately for Lilly, the drug failed its clinical trial shortly after the ad was released (Politico and Eli Lilly 2016). In Croatia, the pharmaceutical company Pliva partnered with *24sata* on a campaign about sex education that was intended to create a broader market for their birth control pill in a country in which birth control had been stigmatized (Eliasson 2017).

Overall, while not as insidious as advertising for the energy industry, health care native advertising still raises a number of issues. Given the role such advertising has played historically in influencing health care policy (Bergan and Risner 2012) and increasing consumer willingness to purchase health care products and services (Kim and Hancock 2017), it is possible that the native format, with its more compelling storytelling and legitimacy bestowed by the host publication, will make the industry's persuasive tool-kit even stronger over time. Native pharmaceutical advertising, moreover, may give the industry an edge in the persistent struggles in the US and the EU to regulate these persuasive effects, as it can indirectly promote new drugs in a manner that evades regulation.

## Issues as "added value" in native advertising

Beyond the health and energy sectors, much issue-based native advertising focuses less on influencing policy than on exploiting a given issue for the advertiser's direct or indirect benefit – in other words, for either a clearly economic benefit or a "mixed" benefit which includes both economic and other factors, such as corporate social responsibility (Drumwright 1996). One common form of issue-based native advertising with a clear economic benefit is a campaign that establishes the advertiser as an expert on a given topic or field through a compelling story in which a company or product plays a heroic role against an emerging threat. As fits its rapidly grow-ing role in the global economy, cybersecurity is a frequent topic of such ads. *The Atlantic* partnered with Booz Allen Hamilton on a cybersecurity piece titled "Stop The Madness" which discussed the vulnerability of the emerging Internet of Things; the campaign included a series of videos about security breaches (Atlantic Re: Think and Booz Allen Hamilton 2017). In *Politico*, a Leidos campaign titled "Ones and Heroes" provided an overview on cyber warfare (Politico and Leidos 2015). Both of these ads worked to convince potential corporate or government customers that the advertiser in question was best positioned to take on the challenge of internet security; in doing so, they portrayed on online world that was increasingly criminal and threatening, navigable only with the help of professionals trained to detect and prevent compromised systems.

While cybersecurity native campaigns tend to foreground the dark underside of technology use, another strain of technology-focused native advertising emphasizes the positive face of technology, placing the advertiser at the center of a technocratic vision of progress. An early example of this was the GE "Look Ahead" campaign, a three-year partnership with *The Economist* that the news magazine described as "an alternative to advertising," featuring daily content associating GE with innovation and global transformation (*Economist* Marketing Solutions n.d.). In a less sweeping but still extensive campaign for Dell in 2016, T Brand Studio ranked 50 cities as "Future Ready Economies" based on their embrace of technology, their maximization of "human capital," and the productivity, growth and innovation in their financial sector. The resulting article, with maps, data, and city profiles, did not focus on the use of Dell technology, but rather celebrated investment in education and physical and digital infrastructure as a route to "future readiness" (T Brand Studio and Dell 2015). The relative weight given to technological innovation, however, is suggested by the fact that Dell chose its own hometown – San Jose – as the world's most future-ready city, despite the region's significant infrastructure and labor inequality issues.

Another T Brand Studio campaign, for USB Warburg Investment Bank, also used the lure of futuristic technology as a means of establishing the advertiser's expertise, celebrating the centenary of Nobel economist and AI pioneer Robert Simon by exploring the potential for AI to take on human attributes. The piece, which begins by inviting readers to have a conversation with a chatbot named Rose, includes a timeline of key events in the history of artificial intelligence and a series of profiles of AI pioneers. The most compelling part of the ad is a short video with Osaka University professor Hiroshi Ishiguro; Ishiguro, who has claimed that his team will create a "conscious" robot by the year 2020, describes his research and wonders whether humans will recognize conscious robots as beings in their own right (T Brand Studio and UBS 2016).

Though these advertisements have as their primary goal the marketing of products and services, not policy advocacy, it is still important to attend to the way in which their framing of technology can both reflect and shape larger cultural ideas about technology use. Technology native advertising presents a contradictory vision of technology – alternately frightening and glorious – but also a consistently deterministic one, in which technology is presented at the cause or solution to social ills and advertisers emerge as the essential mediators of contemporary life. If this does not sound much different from the tone of much technology reporting, that is because, as Sara Watson (2016) has documented, the self-representation of the technology industry has had a long-term shaping effect on technology journalism, helping to marginalize alternative perspectives and critical voices. Native advertising about technology seamlessly integrates with such uncritical technology reporting, making it that much more difficult to imagine different perspectives.

If native ads featuring cutting-edge technologies position advertisers as experts through association, ads which focus on social issues (like the Hyatt ad at the beginning of this chapter) position advertisers as responsible corporate citizens, allowing them to appear to be engaging with contemporary civic debates and potentially working towards a solution to a social problem – even when the advertiser in question is not directly involved in creating or supporting such solutions. Examples of such native campaigns are common in both the US and Europe. Pfizer worked with *The Economist* on a campaign about women with cancer returning to the workforce (Economist Intelligence Unit and Pfizer 2017). A Kohler advertisement in *Mashable* profiled a sanitation nonprofit for World Toilet Day (Mashable and Kohler 2017). Comcast partnered with *Atlantic* on a series called "American Mobility" about the how the lack of access to broadband Internet widens the digital divide (Atlantic Re:Think and Comcast 2017). Campbells worked with *Slate* on a campaign about food sustainability (Slate and Campbells Soup 2017–2018). And in India, the automotive company Mahindra partnered with Newscorp on a campaign that drew attention to issues around child marriage (Newscorp and Mahindra 2015).

Native advertisements such as these have their history in a longer tradition of cause-related marketing that is an appealing yet sometimes risky strategy for advertisers. Scholars of CRM argue that the ads can be seen as exploitative, naïve, or too preachy (Pomering and Johnson 2009; Brønn and Vrioni 2001). Moreover, the recent sharp turn towards populism and nativism around the world has made such seemingly uncontroversial "uplift" advertisements more risky, as they can alienate audiences of a more conservative bent, or be seen by more progressive audiences as exploitative (Wagner and Thompson 1994). A prime example of this in conventional advertising was a 2017 Pepsi commercial in which US celebrity Kylie Jenner offered a police officer a cold can of Pepsi to quell conflict at an unspecified protest march: within hours, the ad had produced such a broad public outcry that it was taken off the air (Victor 2017). Indeed, with that advertisement partly in mind, Hyatt Regency considered pulling their "Story of Hope" advertisement in *The Atlantic* because they worried it would be seen as a statement on white supremacist rallies which had occurred in Charlottesville, Virginia immediately prior to the ad's release (Liffreing 2017).

Underwriting cause-related content can be equally risky for corporations, as it can create the perception of editorial bias in otherwise objective reporting. In 2016, the food conglomerate Mondelez sponsored a *Guardian* column on "sustainable business practices" as a means of giving the conglomerate a greener image. Critics raised a red flag, however, when the column featured a *Guardian* news investigation about child slavery allegations against Nestle – a longtime rival of Mondelez (Schultz 2016). Though *The Guardian* insisted that the article was produced entirely independently, meaning that reporters had proposed the topic, conducted the investigation, and drawn their own conclusions, the resulting flack was damaging both to *The Guardian*, which seemed to be producing advertiser-friendly content, and to Mondelez, whose attempt at "greening" their image was tainted by the perception that they had endorsed a smear against their rival.

## Native advertising and nonprofits: agenda setting and issue framing

Until now, this discussion of issue-based native advertisement has been limited mainly to advertising contracted by for-profit corporations, whether or not such advertising has a clear profit motive. But nonprofit organizations are also increasingly using native advertising, building on a tradition of using paid campaigns to draw awareness to humanitarian crises or social issues that began in the mid-19th century (Ash 2016). Aside from issue awareness, such campaigns are intended to improve a nonprofit's brand identity and, often, to solicit donations (Laidler-Kylander, Quelch and Simonin 2007). As management scholars have documented, nonprofits around the globe have become increasingly business-like in their practices over the past two decades (Maier, Meyer and Steinbereithner 2016), and organizations ranging from Amnesty International to the World Wildlife Foundation now rely heavily on innovative advertising strategies for outreach and fundraising (Ives 2002). Native advertising has been a natural fit, as these charities can frequently provide compelling content for storytelling ads.

At the same time, the use of native advertising by nonprofits and NGOs can also be seen as part of a broader trend toward media-making in the nonprofit/NGO community, in which NGOs provide "boots on the ground" reporting that is then sourced by news outlets whose own reporting resources have been curtailed by budget cuts (Sambrook 2010; Powers 2017). Scholars studying the expansion of NGOs as media providers (Van Leuven and Joye 2014; Powers 2015, 2017) have wondered about the effect of this sourcing on the final editorial product at news outlets and on the overall information environment. While reporting conducted by news-NGO partnerships tends to mimic the tone and form of much mainstream news reporting (Fenton 2010), it has a fundamentally different mission and thus may differ markedly in terms of information framing, blending the informational framing of journalism with the advocacy framing favored by nonprofit groups. In other words, nonprofits may use descriptive strategies that suggest possibilities for action, sometimes with inattentiveness to the root cause of the issue (Powers 2017); additionally, they may make representational choices that amplify the situation to increase engagement. Media scholars have acknowledged the existence of such advocacy frames in conventional journalism practice (Tewksbury et al. 2000; Fisher 2016) but as media organizations increasingly rely on nonprofits, there is potential for journalistic norms to be reshaped (Powers 2015).

This difference in issue framing is greatly amplified when non-profits partner with news outlets on native campaigns. As such campaigns are often designed for marketing or brand recognition, issue-driven native advertising by nonprofits frequently has a secondary framing which places the advertiser in the role of solution provider in order to heighten brand recognition or attract donations (Dorovskykh 2015), much in the way other issue-based native advertising described in this chapter places a for-profit company in a heroic role. This can often reduce the complexity of the issues described. For example, the Bill and Melinda Gates Foundation, which has invested heavily in promoting Common Core standards in US public schools, worked in 2016 with T Brand Studio on a campaign, "Education is Key," that championed Common Core standards and played down the controversy surrounding them by having teachers explain that the controversy was a result of a "shaky rollout." Months later, the Gates Foundation admitted that they had underestimated the challenge of implementing Common Core standards in unprepared states, and backed away from their commitment (Camera 2017). "Education Is Key" remains online as a signpost of the Foundation's effort to present education as a problem that can be "solved" by the Gates' top-down and technocratic approach.

In addition to presenting issues through reductive or skewed frames, non-profit native advertising can shape the news agenda around humanitarian issues in ways that can be both salutary and negative. For example, the UNHCR has partnered with *The Guardian* to produce "Refugee Stories," dramatic, image-driven features about the plight of refugees (*Guardian* and UNHCR 2017). Arguably, these articles could be considered a win-win situation: the *Guardian* gets reportage that aligns with its humanitarian mandate, and the UNHCR draws attention to the refugee crisis and provides positive coverage of refugees to balance out negative media attention (Finnish Institute of London 2017). But it is the UNHCR, not the *Guardian* that is driving the coverage; in effect, the UNHCR thus performs the "agenda setting" role conventionally ascribed to the media. So while such advertisements can potentially expand coverage of underreported crises, they can also draw attention only to crises that NGOs or other nonprofits are directly engaged with, meaning that other kinds of stories might fall by the wayside. As well, if partnerships such as the Guardian/UNHCR sponsorship become more common practice, it is possible that some news outlets will regard such advertisements as sufficient coverage of a situation, deciding that such difficult, resource-intensive stories are beyond their purview.

With these issues in mind, it is troubling that some in the advertising industry see untapped potential in even closer alliances between nonprofits and publications that are "ideologically aligned." An advertising executive argued for such alliances in *Digiday*, suggesting that news publications allow nonprofit to sponsor articles which helped bolster their cause (for example, allowing Planned Parenthood to support articles on abortion rights). As the executive explained, these "seamlessly integrated advocacy opportunities would capitalize on that moment of heightened awareness" (Ipcar 2014).

The notion of "seamlessly integrated advocacy opportunities" suggests a media environment in which, in terms of tone and content, it is in practice quite difficult to know whether one is reading a work of advocacy journalism written by a reporter on assignment, a work of journalism in which the reporter has been paid or sponsored by a nonprofit, or a piece of native advertising written on behalf of the nonprofit. Such an environment would not only reduce trust in the objectivity of journalism – it may also create a backlash (Seu, Flanagan and Orgad 2015), as readers conclude that editorial content intended to stir them to action is just another marketing ploy from a corporatized nonprofit determined to "capitalize on that moment of heightened awareness."

## Native advertising and electoral candidates: uneasy bedfellows

Of all forms of native advertising, political native advertising raises the most immediate set of concerns, as it has potential consequences not only for civic discourse, but for the democratic process itself. As Iversen and Knudsen note in a study of such advertising (2017), native ads for political parties or candidates threaten to erode two separate boundaries that have scaffolded journalistic objectivity – the boundary between editorial and advertising and the boundary between news outlets and political interests. Though the latter boundary is differently permeable in different countries depending on the history of national media institutions (Hallin and Mancini 2004), the availability of objective news coverage of candidates is considered an important part of electoral integrity. The role of traditional political advertising in shaping or even circumventing such coverage has long been a matter of concern for political theorists (Roberts and McCombs 1994; Pfau et al. 2002), and the emergence of political native advertising has sharpened those concerns.

Just as nonprofit native advertising is part of a larger restructuring of how nonprofits use media to further their aims, native political advertising is part of a larger shift in how candidates advertise. Over the past several years, a large share of campaign revenue has shifted onto digital platforms, as politicians have used such platforms to communicate informally with the public in ways that do not resemble conventional advertising (Garrahan 2016), often circumventing regulation in the process (Goodman et al. 2017). This shift has concerned news outlets, which have been searching for a means to make up for the revenue loss and have approached political campaigns with innovative advertising products (Peck 2016).

Once again, the US has been a leader in the tilt towards political native advertising, as the regulatory environment around US political advertising is relatively relaxed. In Europe, political native campaigns are still largely regarded as an unrealized threat on the horizon (Dempsey 2015), though some examples have been noted in Norway (Iversen and Knudsen ibid). Even in the US, however, such advertising has remained relatively limited, in part because candidates have relied heavily on social media and digital platforms to circulate the kinds of messages characteristic of native ads. Yet the scant campaigns that *have* emerged have raised a notable amount of concern, including calls for the U.S. Federal Election Commission (FEC) to regulate such ads closely (Dykhne 2018).

US candidates first began using native advertising as early as 2012, when *BuzzFeed* worked with the Obama campaign on an ad making fun of Republican Presidential candidate Mitt Romney's remark that he had "binders full of women" (Ellis 2012). In 2015, *BuzzFeed* announced that they would pursue native advertising opportunities with political candidates more aggressively, producing video and social media content for candidates in conjunction with *BuzzFeed* Motion Pictures (Murtha and Gourarie 2016), and *Politico* announced a similar push for candidate advertising (Elkin 2016). As the election season began, there were hopes that campaigns would prove – in the words of *BuzzFeed* editor Ben Shapiro – a "massive opportunity" for news publication to experiment with the native format (Ungerleider 2015).

In the end, however, buy-in from candidates was limited. On the Democratic side, the Sanders campaign worked with *Politico* to produce a paid op-ed on the need to eliminate private prisons (*Politico* and Sanders Campaign 2016), and with *BuzzFeed* on a listicle identifying Sanders's strengths (*BuzzFeed* and Sanders Campaign 2016); the Clinton campaign, on the other hand, opted for more conventional advertising on news platforms and an extensive social media presence.[2] Republican candidates did not engage in the practice, though the RNC did sign a $1 million contract with *BuzzFeed* that might have resulted in native advertising had it been completed. In an indication of the complexity of the decision-making around such ads, *BuzzFeed* announced in 2016 that they faced an editorial and ethical dilemma after the nomination of Donald Trump as the Republican candidate, and were cancelling their advertising relationship with the RNC (Kaufman 2016). The cancellation led some media observers to wonder whether *BuzzFeed's* enthusiasm for political advertising had been tempered by the realities of political campaigning – and by the realization that such advertising might undermine their own political coverage (Carpentier 2016). This supposition is borne out by Iversen and Knudsen (ibid), whose study of responses to political native advertising in Norway found that the presence of political native advertising in news outlets reduced reader's overall trust in political news, even when they were able to clearly distinguish such ads.

## Conclusion

A 2017 survey of native advertising trends in the news media produced for the International News Media Association includes a case study of a Swedish paper, *Helsingsborg Dagblad*, that entered into a native advertising partnership with its own local government (Laursen and INMA 2017). The Helsingborg City Council hired the outlet's brand studio to provide local coverage of community affairs as advertisements, including feature stories and videos. The case study emphasized that *Helsingsborg Dagblad's* editor approved the advertising content before publication, in order to avoid conflicts between the paper's editorial coverage of local affairs and the advertisements in question (Laursen and INMA 2017), and discussed the campaign enthusiastically as an experiment in community engagement for the newspaper.

Though it is tempting to think of this experiment as an example of government "investment" in local news coverage – and thus a positive step towards funding community journalism – what *Helsingsborg Dagblad* and the city of Helsingsborg are doing is something quite different. It is difficult to read through the study without wondering about the effect on civic life of reading local news largely written through the filter of a native content studio. Aside from the obvious propaganda implications, such an approach suggests a re-articulation of the role of the newspaper within the community, a shift away from civic responsibility in the name of commercial survival. Even if a news editor is vigilant about avoiding the appearance of conflict, an advertorial approach to civic news, drawing on the tendency of advertising to "soothe and divert" (Lewis 2016, 96) has the potential to undercut adjacent editorial content containing more serious forms of critique.

Over the course of this chapter, I have demonstrated that issue-based native advertising now plays a prominent role in the revenue models of news content studios, especially at news outlets reaching affluent and influential audiences in the US and Europe. I have pointed to various "trouble spots" in the rise of such advertising, including the increased ability of such ads to persuade media audiences because of their storytelling strategies and the legitimacy they borrow from the news outlets that display them. In the words of legal scholar Amar Bakshi:

> there is a consumer deception that does not pertain to a particular product, service, or brand, but rather to the interests of consumers writ large debating issues of public import . . . When [policy focused] advertising campaigns are presented as native ads, they can acquire the patina or independence and respectability of the host publication. Consumers may assume that the editors and journalists at a publication sincerely believe a given policy position, and therefore be more willing to accept that the position best serves the interest of consumers.
>
> (Bakshi 2015)

Despite the justifiable concern these advertisements provoke, they remain difficult to regulate, precisely because – as Bakshi points out – institutional advertising often does not pertain to a particular product, service or brand. This means such advertising is not subject to the same regulations as ordinary consumer advertising: in the US, it also means it has the additional protections accorded to corporate speech in the US legal system.

This is, to say the least, unfortunate. Whether in the US or Europe, issue-based native ads are fertile grounds for the unchecked amplification of commercial speech. It is not just that such advertisements allow corporations to tell readers what to think, what to do, and who to vote for; it is that they can ultimately distort a news outlet's own sense of what voices should be heard, what topics should be addressed, and what messages should prevail. At worst, they accelerate the neoliberal "enclosure" of the media within the structure of the market (Hallin 2008) limiting the ability of the media to shape civil society by framing public debate and democratic participation as anything other than the function of the market (King, Schneer, and White 2017). Media organizations which engage in this practice need to think beyond the concept of editorial conflict when taking on issue-based campaigns, to ensure that those who need to communicate with the public without the mediation of advertising are not increasingly marginalized.

## Notes

1  In another recent incident which raised the specter of pay-to-play, the well-regarded US magazine *Texas Monthly* entered into a different sort of "partnership"

relationship with the dating service Bumble, agreeing to write a story about the site in response for promotion of the magazine on Bumble's platform (Nelson 2017). In this incident, it is unclear who is the advertiser and who is the client; the result, however, was a compromised article.

2  Clinton was, however, the topic of a native ad in the lead-up to the elections. Perhaps regrettably in hindsight, Blackberry created a native ad based on the Hillary Clinton email controversy in 2015, running an article in *Variety* titled "Hillary Clinton's E-mail: Lessons Learned" (Schwartz 2015).

## Bibliography

Atlantic Re:Think and Athena. 2017. "A Mission to Heal." *The Atlantic*. www.theatlantic.com/sponsored/athena-2017/a-mission-to-heal/1371/.

Atlantic Re:Think and AT&T. 2017. "Crisis Converted: Cybersecurity." *The Atlantic*. www.theatlantic.com/sponsored/att-2017/crisis-converted/1446/.

Atlantic Re:Think and Booz Allen Hamilton. 2017. "Stop the Madness: Real Security for a Connected World." *The Atlantic*. www.theatlantic.com/sponsored/booz-allen-hamilton-2017/stop-the-madness-real-security-for-a-connected-world/.

Atlantic Re:Think and Comcast. 2017. "The Limits of Mobile-Only Internet Access." *The Atlantic*. www.theatlantic.com/sponsored/comcast-2017/limits-of-mobile-only-internet-access/1491/.

Atlantic Re:Think and Hewlett Packard. 2017. "Eighteen Zeros." *The Atlantic*. www.theatlantic.com/sponsored/hpe-2017/eighteen-zeros/1545/?utm_source=FB_AR_O_1545_1.

Atlantic Re:Think and Hyatt. 2017. "Speaking of Hope." *The Atlantic*. www.theatlantic.com/sponsored/hyatt-2017/speaking-of-hope/1452/.

Atlantic Re:Think and Novo Nordisk. 2017. "An Emergency in Slow Motion." *The Atlantic*. www.theatlantic.com/sponsored/novo-nordisk-2017/an-emergency-in-slow-motion/1605/.

Ash, S. 2016. *Funding Philanthropy: Dr. Barnardo, Metaphor, Narrative and Spectacle*. Cambridge: Oxford University Press.

Bakshi, A. C. 2015. "Why and How to Regulate Native Advertising in Online News Publications." *University of Baltimore Journal of Media Law and Ethics* 4, no. 4: 4–47.

Barnouw, E. 1978. *The Sponsor: Notes on a Modern Potentate*. Vol. 580. Piscataway, NJ: Transaction Publishers.

BBC StoryWorks and Microsoft. 2016. "Laptop Learning for Success." *BBC News*. www.bbc.com/storyworks/future/future-ready/laptop-learning-for-success.

Bell, E. 2017. "Silicon Valley Helped Russia Sway the US Election: So Now What?" *The Guardian*, October 29, 2017. www.theguardian.com/media/2017/oct/29/media-symbiotic-relationship-facebook-worry-democracy.

Bergan, D. and Risner, G. 2012. "Issue Ads and the Health Reform Debate." *Journal of Health Politics, Policy and Law* 37, no. 3: 513–549.

BG Brand Lab and Pfizer, 2017. "Dear Scientist." http://sponsored.bostonglobe.com/pfizer/.

Bloomberg and Optum. 2017. "Day Zero." *Bloomberg*. www.bloomberg.com/news/sponsors/features/optum/day-zero/?adv=7641&prx_t=468CAegEOAXikPA.

Bodkin, C. D., Amato, L. H. and Amato, C. H. 2015. "The Influence of Green Advertising during a Corporate Disaster." *Corporate Communications: An International Journal* 20, no. 3: 256–275.

Brønn, P. S. and Vrioni, A. B. 2001. "Corporate Social Responsibility and Cause-Related Marketing: An Overview." *International Journal of Advertising* 20, no. 2: 207–222.

Brown, C. and Waltzer, H. 2005. "Every Thursday: Advertorials by Mobil Oil on the Op-Ed Page of The New York Times." *Public Relations Review* 31, no. 2: 197–208.

BuzzFeed and Bernie Sanders' Campaign. 2016. "15 Reasons Bernie Sanders Is the Candidate We've Been Waiting For." *BuzzFeed*, January 8, 2016. www.buzzfeed.com/berniesanders/times-bernie-sanders-gave-us-all-hope?utm_term=.ckmLKqqN8k#.mh9l4mmvw2.

Camera, L. 2017. "Gates Foundation Backs Away from Common Core, Pledges 1.7 Billion to Build Network of Schools." *Technocracy News*, October 19, 2017. www.technocracy.news/index.php/2017/10/19/gates-foundation-pledges-1-7-billion/.

Carpentier, M. 2016. "BuzzFeed Cancelling RNC Ads Masks the Issue: Sponsored Content for Politicians." *The Guardian*, June 6, 2016. www.theguardian.com/media/2016/jun/06/buzzfeed-donald-trump-native-advertising-political-candidates.

Cooper, C. A. and Nownes, A. J. 2004. "Money Well Spent? An Experimental Investigation of the Effects of Advertorials on Citizen Opinion." *American Politics Research* 32, no. 5: 546–569.

Dempsey, S. 2015. "Could Native Advertising Get Political?" *The Independent* (Ireland), November 1, 2015. www.independent.ie/business/technology/news/could-native-advertising-get-political-or-has-it-already-34158685.html.

Donohue, J. 2006. "A History of Drug Advertising: The Evolving Roles of Consumers and Consumer Protection." *The Milbank Quarterly* 84, no. 4: 659–699.

Dorovskykh, O. 2015. "Native Advertising as a Storytelling Tool: Framing of Brand Messages." Masters diss., University of Missouri-Columbia.

Drumwright, M. E. 1996. "Company Advertising with a Social Dimension: The Role of Noneconomic Criteria." *The Journal of Marketing* 60, no. 4: 71–87.

Dykhne, I. 2018. "Persuasion or Deception? Native Advertising in Political Campaigns." *Southern California Law Review* 91, no. 2 (January). https://southerncalifornialawreview.com/2018/01/01/persuasive-or-deceptive-native-advertising-in-political-campaigns-note-by-irina-dykhne/#_ftn183.

Economist Intelligence Unit and Gilead. 2017. "White Paper: Access to Healthcare." *The Economist*, June 29, 2017. www.eiu.com/industry/article/1115633095/white-paper-access-to-healthcare/2017-06-29.

Economist Intelligence Unit and Cigna. 2017. "Tackling the Opioid Crisis: Views on Effective Approaches to Treatment." *The Economist*. http://tacklingopioids.eiu.com.

Economist Intelligence Unit and Pfizer. 2017. "The Road to a Better Normal: Breast Cancer Patients and Survivors in the EU Workforce." *The Economist*, October 10, 2017. http://perspectives.eiu.com/healthcare/road-better-normal-breast-cancer-patients-and-survivors-eu-workforce.

Economist Marketing Solutions. n.d. "GE Look Ahead." *The Economist*. https://marketingsolutions.economist.com/work/general-electric.

Eliasson, J. 2017. "How Pharma Company Promoted the Pill in Croatia by Educating about Safe Sex." *Native Advertising Institute*, December 6, 2017. https://nativeadvertisinginstitute.com/blog/pharma-company-educating-safe-sex/.

Elkin, T. 2016. "Politico Focus Aims to Connect Brands with Political Influencers." *MediaPost*, November 30, 2016. www.mediapost.com/publications/article/290004/politico-focus-aims-to-connect-brands-with-politic.html.

Ellis, J. 2012. "BuzzFeed Adapts Its Branded Content Approach to Political Advertising, and Obama's In." *NiemanLab*, October 14, 2012. www.niemanlab.org/2012/10/buzzfeed-adapts-its-branded-content-approach-to-political-advertising-and-obamas-in.

EPRA. 2006. "Political Advertising: Case Studies and Monitoring." *EPRA*, May 17, 2006. https://epra3-production.s3.amazonaws.com/. . ./files/. . ./Political_advertising_final.doc.

ExxonMobil. 2000. "2000 ExxonMobil Global Climate Change Op-Ed Series: Climate Files." *Climate Files*. www.climatefiles.com/exxonmobil/2000-exxon-global-climate-change-op-ed-series/.

Fenton, N. 2010. *New Media, Old News: Journalism and Democracy in the Digital Age*. Thousand Oaks, CA: Sage Publications.

The Finnish Institute in London. 2017. *Refugees and Asylum Seekers in Press Coverage*. www.fininst.uk/wp-content/uploads/2017/11/Refugees_and_asylum_seekers_in_press_coverage.pdf.

Fisher, C. 2016. "The Advocacy Continuum: Towards a Theory of Advocacy in Journalism." *Journalism* 17, no. 6: 711–726.

Frosch, D., Krueger, P., Hornik, R., Cronholm, P. and Barg, F. K. 2007. "Creating demand for prescription drugs: a content analysis of television direct-to-consumer advertising." *The Annals of Family Medicine* 5, no. 1: 6–13.

Funk, M. 2016. "Did Exxon Lie about Global Warming?" *Rolling Stone*, June 30, 2016. www.rollingstone.com/politics/news/did-exxon-lie-about-global-warming-20160630.

Garrahan, M. 2016. "Political Advertising: An Industry in Peril." *Financial Times*, October 28, 2016. www.ft.com/content/a81db6de-9c1b-11e6-8324-be63473ce146.

Glenzian, J. 2017. "Nestle Pays $200 a Year to Bottle Water Near Flint: Where Water Is Undrinkable." *The Guardian*, September 29, 2017. www.theguardian.com/us-news/2017/sep/29/nestle-pays-200-a-year-to-bottle-water-near-flint-where-water-is-undrinkable.

Goodman, E., Labo, S., Tambini, D. and Moore, M. 2017. *The New Political Campaigning*. London: LSE Reprints. http://eprints.lse.ac.uk/71945/7/LSE%20MPP%20Policy%20Brief%2019%20-%20The%20new%20political%20campaigning_final.pdf.

Guardian Studio and UNHCR. 2017. "UNHCR: Refugee Stories." *The Guardian*. www.theguardian.com/unhcr-refugee-stories.

Guardian Studio and UNHCR. 2016. "From Africa to Australia: The Long Journey of a Refugee." *The Guardian*, May 17, 2016. www.theguardian.com/unhcr-refugee-stories/2016/may/18/from-africa-to-australia-the-long-journey-of-a-refugee.

Haley, E. 1996. "Exploring the Construct of Organization as Source: Consumers' Understandings of Organizational Sponsorship of Advocacy Advertising." *Journal of Advertising* 25, no. 2: 19–35.

Hallin, D. C. 2008. "Neoliberalism, social movements and change in media systems in the late twentieth century." *The media and social theory*: 43–58.

Hallin, D. C. and Mancini, P. 2004. *Comparing Media Systems: Three Models of Media and Politics*. Cambridge: Cambridge University Press.

Ipcar, M. 2014. "Publishers: 'Look beyond Native Advertising to Native Advocacy'." *Digiday*, August 19, 2014. https://digiday.com/media/publishers-look-beyond-native-advertising-native-advocacy/.

Iversen, M. H. and Knudsen, E. 2017. "When Politicians Go Native: The Consequences of Political Native Advertising for Citizens' Trust in News." *Journalism* (January).

Ives, N. 2002. "Unions and Advocacy Groups Are Putting a Madison Avenue Finesse on Their Protest Ads." *New York Times*, December 26, 2002. www.nytimes.com/2002/12/26/business/media-business-advertising-unions-advocacy-groups-are-putting-madison-avenue.html.

Kaufman, G. 2016. "Buzzfeed Break RNC's Ad Deal: Could It Affect Trump's Campaign?" *The Christian Science Monitor*, June 7, 2016. www.csmonitor.com/USA/Politics/2016/0607/Buzzfeed-breaks-RNC-ad-deal-Could-it-affect-Trump-s-campaign.

Kim, B.-H., Pasadeos, Y. and Barban, A. 2001. "On the Deceptive Effectiveness of Labeled and Unlabeled Advertorial Formats." *Mass Communication & Society* 4, no. 3: 265–281.

Kim, S. J. and Hancock, J. T. 2017. "How Advertorials Deactivate Advertising Schema: MTurk-Based Experiments to Examine Persuasion Tactics and Outcomes in Health Advertisements." *Communication Research* 44, no. 7: 1019–1045.

King, G., Schneer, B. and White, A. 2017. "How the News Media Activate Public Expression and Influence National Agendas." *Science* 358, no. 6364: 776–780.

Kotler, P. and Zaltman, G. 1971. "Social Marketing: An Approach to Planned Social Change." *Journal of Marketing* 35, no. 3 (July): 3–12.

Laidler-Kylander, N., Quelch, J. A. and Simonin, B. L. 2007. "Building and Valuing Global Brands in the Nonprofit Sector." *Nonprofit Management and Leadership* 17, no. 3 (March): 253–277.

Laufer, W. S. 2003. "Social Accountability and Corporate Greenwashing." *Journal of Business Ethics* 43, no. 3: 253–261.

Laursen, J. and INMA. 2017. "Native Advertising Trends in the News Industry." *The Native Advertising Institute*. https://nativeadvertisinginstitute.com/wp-content/uploads/2017/12/inma_2017NativeAdvertising.pdf.

Leonardo, A. T., Mantel-Teeuwisse, A. K., Paschke, A., Leufkens, H. G. M., Puil, L., Poplavska, E. and Mintzes, B. 2007. "Unbranded Advertising of Prescription Medicines to the Public by Pharmaceutical Companies (Protocol)." *Cochrane Database of Systematic Reviews*, no. 7.

Lewis, J. 2016. "The Commercial Constraints on Speech Limit Democratic Debate." In *Blurring the Lines: Market-Driven and Democracy-Driven Freedom of Expression*, edited by M. Edström, A. T. Kenyon, and E.-M. Svensson. Gothenberg: Nordicom.

Liffreing, I. 2017. "Hyatt Deliberated Scrapping Its New Branded-Content Work after Charlottesville Riots." *Digiday*, August 17, 2017. https://digiday.com/marketing/hyatt-deliberated-scrapping-new-branded-content-work-charlottesville-riots/?utm_content=buffer48f6e&utm_medium=social&utm_source=twitter.com&utm_campaign=buffer.

Maier, F., Meyer, M. and Steinbereithner, M. 2016. "Nonprofit Organizations becoming Business-Like: A Systematic Review." *Nonprofit and Voluntary Sector Quarterly* 45, no. 1: 64–86.

Marchand, R. 1987. "The Fitful Career of Advocacy Advertising: Political Protection, Client Cultivation, and Corporate Morale." *California Management Review* 29, no. 2 (Winter): 128–156.

Mashable Brand Studio and Kohler. 2017. "This Organization Uses Human-Centered Design to Deliver Impactful Sanitation Solutions (Paid Content by Kohler)." *Mashable*, October 31, 2017. https://mashable.com/2017/10/31/ide-global-sanitation-solutions/.

Meadow, R. G. 1981. "The Political Advertising Dimensions of Nonproduct Advertising." *Journal of Communication* 31, no. 3: 69–82.

Meenaghan, T. 2001. "Understanding Sponsorship Effects." *Psychology and Marketing* 18, no. 2 (January): 95–122.

Morrell, G. 2014. "No, BP Didn't Ruin the Gulf." *Politico*, October 21. www.politico.com/magazine/story/2014/10/gulf-coast-recovery-expectations-112088?o=1.

Murphy, C. 2002. "Is BP beyond Petroleum? Hardly." *Fortune*, September 30, 2002. http://archive.fortune.com/magazines/fortune/fortune_archive/2002/09/30/329277/index.htm.

Murtha, J. and Gourarie, C. 2016. "Do BuzzFeed's Native Political Ads Cross a Line?" *Columbia Journalism Review*. www.cjr.org/analysis/a_major_player_in_the.php.

Neason, A. 2018. "*Texas Monthly* EIC Wanders into an Ethical Gray Zone." *Columbia Journalism Review*, January 26, 2018. www.cjr.org/business_of_news/texas-monthly-bumble.php.

Nelson, G. 2017. "I'm a Guy Who Makes Branded Content: We Can Make It Better." *Vox Media*, October 16, 2017. www.voxmedia.com/about-vox-media/2017/10/16/16473532/im-a-guy-who-makes-branded-content-we-can-make-it-better.

NewsCorp Studios and Mahindra. 2015. "How Schools Can Save a Girl from Child Marriage." *NewsCorpStudios*. https://readymag.com/NewsCorpStudios/MahindraMediaKit/10/.

Peck, G. A. 2016. "As Political Ad Spending Increases, Newspapers Need a Plan of Action." *Editor and Publisher*, February 1, 2016. www.editorandpublisher.com/feature/as-political-ad-spending-increases-newspapers-need-a-plan-of-action.

Pfau, M., Holbert, R. L., Szabo, E. A. and Kaminski, K. 2002. "Issue-Advocacy versus Candidate Advertising: Effects on Candidate Preferences and Democratic Process." *Journal of Communication* 52, no. 2: 301–315.

Politico Focus and British Petroleum. 2017. "Sponsored Content: Explore How BP Uses VR to Train Offshore Teams." *Politico*. www.politico.com/sponsor-content/2017/1/360-of-safety.

Politico Focus and Pfizer. 2017. "Sponsored Content: Harnessing Innovation to Shape Health Care Policies That Matter." *Politico*, October 4, 2017. www.politico.com/sponsor-content/2017/10/04/harnessing-innovation-to-shape-health-care-policies-that-matter?.

Politico Focus and Eli Lilly. 2016. "Alzheimer's Science Is Changing, Can Policy Catch Up?" *Politico*. www.politico.com/sponsor-content/2016/08/alzheimers-science-is-changing?cid201608hp.

Politico Focus and Sanders Campaign. 2016. "We Must End for-Profit Prisons." *Politico*. February 26, 2016. www.politico.com/sponsor-content/2016/02/we-must-end-for-profit-prisons.

Politico Focus and American Cancer Society. 2015. "Light a Candle." *Politico*. http://focus.politico.com.

Politico Focus and Leidos. 2015. "Ones and Heroes: A Briefing on Cyber Warfare." *Politico*. www.politico.com/sponsor-content/2015/12/ones-and-heroes?cid=2015 12ldhp.

Pomering, A. and Johnson, L. W. 2009. "Advertising Corporate Social Responsibility Initiatives to Communicate Corporate Image: Inhibiting Scepticism to Enhance Persuasion." *Corporate Communications: An International Journal* 14, no. 4: 420–439.

Powers, M. 2017. "Beyond Boon or Bane: Using Normative Theories to Evaluate the Newsmaking Efforts of NGOs." *Journalism Studies* 18, no. 9: 1070–1086.

Powers, M. 2015. "The New Boots on the Ground: NGOs in the Changing Landscape of International News." *Journalism* 17, no. 4: 401–416.

Roberts, M. and McCombs, M. 1994. "Agenda Setting and Political Advertising: Origins of the News Agenda." *Political Communication* 11, no. 3: 249–262.

Sambrook, R. 2010. *Are Foreign Correspondents Redundant? The Changing Face of International News*. Oxford: Reuters Institute for the Study of Journalism.

Schudson, M. 2011. *The Sociology of News*. New York, NY: Norton.

Schultz, E. J. 2016. "This Negative Story Is Brought to You by . . . Mondelez?" *Advertising Age*, February 1, 2016. http://adage.com/article/media/negative-story-nestle-brought-mondelez/302461/.

Schumann, D. W., Hathcote, J. M. and Susan W. 1991. "Corporate advertising in America: A review of published studies on use, measurement, and effectiveness." *Journal of Advertising* 20, no. 3: 35–56.

Schwartz, H. 2015. "Hillary Clinton's email Controversy Is Being Used as a Native Ad for Blackberry." *The Washington Post*, April 2, 2015. www.washingtonpost.com/news/the-fix/wp/2015/04/02/hillary-clintons-e-mail-scandal-is-being-used-as-a-native-ad-about-blackberry/?utm_term=.0bf782afe885.

Sethi, S. P. 1978. "Advocacy Advertising: The American Experience." *California Management Review* 21, no. 1: 55–68.

Seu, I. B., Flanagan, F. and Orgad, S. 2015 "The Good Samaritan and the Marketer: Public Perceptions of Humanitarian and International Development NGOs." *International Journal of Nonprofit and Voluntary Sector Marketing* 20, no. 3: 211–225.

Slate and Campbells Soup. 2017–2018. "How Do We Feed a Growing Population?" *Slate*. http://partners.slate.com/campbells-uncanned-how-do-we-feed-a-growing-population/.

Smith, K., Taken, L. Smith, M. and Dunbar, S. 2014. "Using Corporate Advertising to Improve Public Perception of Energy Companies." *Journal of Strategic Marketing* 22, no. 4: 347–356.

Solman, G. 2008. "BP: Coloring Public Opinion?" *Adweek*, January 14, 2008. www.adweek.com/brand-marketing/bp-coloring-public-opinion-91662/.

Starr, J. M. 2001. *Air Wars: The Fight to Reclaim Public Broadcasting*. Philadelphia: Temple University Press.

Supran, G. and Oreskes, N. 2017. "Assessing ExxonMobil's Climate Change Communications 1977–2014." *Environmental Research Letters* 12. http://iopscience.iop.org/article/10.1088/1748-9326/aa815f/pdf.

T Brand Studio and Chevron. 2016. "A Complex Flow of Energy." *New York Times*. https://paidpost.nytimes.com/chevron/a-complex-flow-of-energy.html#.WXKZXq2ZNmA.

T Brand Studio and Nestle. 2017. "Working together for Water." *New York Times*, October 24, 2017. https://paidpost.nytimes.com/nestle-waters/working-together-for-water.html.

T Brand Studio and Statoil. 2017. "A Different Look at Energy." *New York Times*. https://paidpost.nytimes.com/statoil/a-different-look-at-energy.html.

T Brand Studio and Gates Foundation. 2016. "The Gates Foundation Presents: Education Is Key." *T Brand Studio Vimeo Page*, October 25, 2017. https://vimeo.com/167752657.

T Brand Studio and Shell. 2015. "Powering Human Progress." *New York Times*. https://paidpost.nytimes.com/shell/powering-human-progress.html.

T Brand Studio and Statoil. 2016. "A Different Look at Energy Progress." *New York Times*. https://paidpost.nytimes.com/statoil/a-different-look-at-energy.html.

T Brand Studio and UBS. 2016. "What It Takes to Be Human." *New York Times*, June 14, 2016. https://paidpost.nytimes.com/ubs/what-it-takes-to-be-human.html.

T Brand Studio and Dell. 2015. "Study: San Jose Metro Area Leads U.S. in Future Readiness." *New York Times*, October 19, 2015. https://paidpost.nytimes.com/dell/future-ready-economies/study-san-jose-metro-area-leads-us-in-future-readiness.html.

T Brand Studio and Shell. 2014. "Cities Energized." *New York Times*, November 18, 2014. https://paidpost.nytimes.com/shell/cities-energized.html.

Teicher, J. 2017. "Should Pharmaceutical Companies Be Allowed to Do Content Marketing?" *Contently*, April 21, 2017. https://contently.com/strategist/2017/04/21/should-pharmaceutical-companies-be-allowed-to-do-content-marketing/.

Tewksbury, D., Jones, J., Peske, M. W., Raymond, A. and Vig, W. 2000. "The Interaction of News and Advocate Frames: Manipulating Audience Perceptions of a Local Public Policy Issue." *Journalism & Mass Communication Quarterly* 77, no. 4: 804–829.

Ungerleider, N. 2015. "BuzzFeed to Produce Native Political Advertising." *Fast Company*, October 12, 2015. www.fastcompany.com/3052182/buzzfeed-ramps-up-native-political-advertising.

Van Leuven, S. and Joye, S. 2014. "Civil Society Organizations at the Gates? A Gatekeeping Study of News Making Efforts by NGOs and Government Institutions." *The International Journal of Press/Politics* 19, no. 2: 160–180.

Victor, D. 2017. "Pepsi Pulls Ad Accused of Trivializing Black Lives Matter." *New York Times*, April 5, 2017. www.nytimes.com/2017/04/05/business/kendall-jenner-pepsi-ad.html?mtrref=www.google.com&gwh=71C457CAC70AB3CF0 A0A27BBCB669ED4&gwt=pay.

Vizard, S. 2015. "The NHS Hopes Joining Forces with Tinder Will Help It 'Normalize' Organ Donation." *Marketing Week*, December 14, 2015. www. marketingweek.com/2015/12/14/the-nhs-hopes-joining-forces-with-tinder-help-can-normalise-organ-donation/.

Voorhees, J. 2013. "The Atlantic Yanks Scientology Advertorial After Outcry." *Slate*, January 15, 2013. www.slate.com/blogs/the_slatest/2013/01/15/the_atlantic_ scientology_magazine_yanks_sponsored_content_after_outcry.html.

Wagner, L. and Thompson, R. L. 1994. "Cause-related marketing: Fundraising tool or phony philanthropy." *Nonprofit World* 12, no. 6: 9–13.

Waltzer, H. 1988. "Corporate Advocacy Advertising and Political Influence." *Public Relations Review* 14, no. 1 (Spring): 41–55.

Washington Post Brand Studio and Battelle. "Emerging Threats." *The Washington Post*, May 22, 2017. www.washingtonpost.com/sf/brand-connect/battelle/ emerging-threats/.

Washington Post Brand Studio and American Fuel and Petrochemical Manufacturers. "Oil Refiners and Petrochemical Producers Are Critical in the Drive to Save Energy." *The Washington Post*, March 19, 2017. www.washingtonpost.com/sf/ brand-connect/AFPM/oil-refiners-and-petrochemical-producers-are-critical-in-the-drive-to-save-energy/.

Watson, S. M. "Toward a Constructive Technology Criticism." *Columbia Journalism Review*, October 4, 2016. www.cjr.org/tow_center_reports/constructive_ technology_criticism.php.

Wemple, E. 2014. "Politico Magazine Makes Space for BP Corporate Flack." *The Washington Post*, October 22, 2014. www.washingtonpost.com/blogs/erik-wemple/wp/2014/10/22/politico-magazine-makes-space-for-bp-corporate-flack/?utm_term=.7689934ab446.

West, D. M., Heith, D. and Goodwin, C. 1996. "Harry and Louise Go to Washington: Political Advertising and Health Care Reform." *Journal of Health Politics, Policy, and Law* 21, no. 1: 35–68.

Zeigler, J. A. 1970. "Social Change through Issue Advertising." *Sociological Inquiry* 40, no. 1 (January): 159–165.

# 4 Going native at *The New York Times*

## A case study

*Ava Sirrah*

*This case study, written by a former employee of T Brand Studios, provides an industry-side look at the* Times' *transition to native advertising, as well as broader observations about challenges faced by the industry as it moves forward.*

"We cannot be in the business of dying a slower death than other news publishers." This was the mantra of Meredith Levien, the Chief Revenue Officer at *The New York Times*. Mrs. Levien repeated these words during every quarterly sales meeting held on the 15th floor of *The New York Times* building. Nearly every time she said this, the sales staff shuddered. The sales department had built their entire careers by selling prints ads to advertisers who never questioned the value of the medium. Mrs. Levien's words struck them not as a natural evolution of their job description, but rather as a threat to everything they knew about newspaper ad placement. Their department was about to get gutted and reimagined as an advertising agency.

From the very beginning of Levien's tenure at the Times, sales people at the company were not sure what to make of the changes she mandated. She was asking people who were used to selling ad space to start selling ideas. The legacy paper was trying to shift their value proposition overnight by mimicking what they saw successful ad agencies do: sell creative campaigns. In this process, *the Times* started using the language of Madison Avenue marketers; content marketing and storytelling became buzzwords. By copying what they saw, *the Times* hoped to secure multi-million-dollar brand budgets.

This chapter highlights how native ads came to represent the white knight news publishers were looking for as traditional forms of advertising revenue declined. It captures how native ads are produced in T Brand Studio, the branded content arm of *the Times*. The examples presented illuminate the precarious position of all news publishers when they try to earn advertising revenue by selling their branded content services. Traditional ad agencies still have an advantage when it comes to securing million-dollar budgets from brands since they have long-standing relationships with clients; T Brand, by contrast, has to leverage the content and skills of their newsroom to stay competitive in the marketplace. Therefore, senior management has created a culture that actively muddies the line between editorial and branded content, even as they publicly maintain the importance of keeping each distinct. This chapter acts less as a critique of T Brand Studio's particular approach than as a look at some of the challenges all publishers confront as they try to expand their native advertising divisions.

I joined *the Times'* branded content studio, T Brand, one year after its inception in 2014. Previously, I was working at the advertising agency BBDO as a digital strategist. Six months before my first day at the paper, another marketing specialist was hired as *the Times'* first creative media strategist, placed within a now extinct department called Sales Development. This employee's professional background, like mine, was at a creative ad agency. Previous to joining the paper they worked as a copywriter at a large ad agency. The first creative strategist found the job through LinkedIn while the website's filters were intentionally set to look for open positions in the advertising industry. Both of us saw *the Times* logo pop up on our job search and thought it sounded like a new and exciting opportunity.

The job was exciting, but not in the ways either of us could have predicted. In an interview I conducted with this employee after they left *the Times*, they said, "In hindsight, I was probably naive about what a shift to a publisher would mean . . . I didn't quite understand the realities of working at a publisher" (Sirrah personal interview 2016). This statement is indicative of the drastic cultural change the paper was undergoing. *The Times* wanted the perspective and experience of fresh young talent to rub off on veterans at the company. The new positions the paper created and filled injected a valuable marketing skill set to the company that previously did not have to worry about selling creative ideas to clients. *The Times'* 2014 innovation report highlighted why they needed to change titles to attract fresh talent, acknowledging that "digital staffers want to play creative roles, not service roles" (The New York Times 2014). Previously, roles in the advertising department were worded as positions that support the sales staff. As an employee noted in the same report, "Young digital talent is rarely motivated by money. Typically they are motivated by the potential to make impact at an organization that speaks to their values. This is the NYT trump card and should be played as often as possible" (Times 2014). With a mission to attract young digital talent, *the Times* went to work and hoped that with title changes and a hiring spree they could reinvent themselves.

Before 2014, the publishers' main priority, when it came to advertising, was buttressing its sales staff. The sales team was responsible for the majority of the paper's revenue, and they were used to meeting their quarterly earning goals by selling print and digital ad space. Two decades ago, the sales team generated 63 percent of the paper's revenue. Today, subscriptions account for 61 percent and advertising represents 33 percent of their total revenue (Kafka 2017). When print was the primary channel for reading the news, a beauty brand like Lancome would run a full page ad adjacent to the day's biggest headlines, and it was sure to get engaged eyeballs.

As the number of media channels grew, readership for many news publishers decreased (Barthel 2017). The paper could no longer go to their most loyal clients and use high readership figures to convince them to spend their ad dollars with *the Times*. Therefore, the sales team had a harder time meeting their revenue goals. They also had to deal with clients who had begun to want a mix of media platforms to promote their products; marketers realized they could spend less in print, capture their target audience, and create digital content to run on new media channels. Finally, the sales division was crippled by the ineffectiveness of *the Times'* digital ad format; like most newspapers, their digital display ads had an average click-through-rate of only .05 percent (Chaffey 2017). Clicks on these ad units were rare since readers had limited patience for interruptive pop-up ads. Media fragmentation paired with what readers demanded of news publishers set the scene for *The New York Times'* new investment, T Brand Studio.

### *The Times'* new sales pitch

By the time I was hired at *the Times*, the paper had found their new direction: as other outlets embraced native advertising, they had become convinced that storytelling was the way out of their present crisis. Over the past decade, both news outlets and advertisers had built up something of a cult around the idea of "storytelling," recognizing it as a highly coveted skill. Storytelling is defined in many different ways by marketers, but its core mission is the same: creating compelling narratives around a product or service. The practice is rooted in wedding a brand to a topic people already care about. Increasingly, marketers have come to understand that content leading with a brand's attributes will not grab people's interest, but rather brands should find ways to make themselves relevant to what people are already gravitating towards (Nieman Newswire 2015). Joe Pulizzi, the founder of Content Marketing Institute, has even said, "Whether the brand goals are rooted in search engine optimization (getting found), lead generation (conversion) or leveraging social media tools, none of them will be effective without compelling storytelling" (Pulizzi 2012). The industry has attached itself to content marketing, the idea that a product or service should be wedded to content for which people already show an affinity. By

2014, it became clear that this was more than a fleeting trend since clients consistently asked for branded content. Storytelling was a skill T Brand Studio had mastered and therefore could charge advertisers for. After all, the newsroom creates compelling stories that millions of people want to read every day; why shouldn't their advertising department be able to do the same thing? Hence, T Brand's slogan became "Stories That Influence The influential" (T Brand 2018). Their sizzle reel emphasizes the newsroom's role in inspiring branded content and has vignettes that shift back and forth from visuals the newsroom created for editorial articles, and those that are produced by T Brand for advertisers (T Brand 2018). This is the sales pitch that drove many client meetings where creative strategists (myself included) told clients that they knew what stories people pay attention to and with the right budget they could help them tell their brand story too.

To fully understand why storytelling gained traction and became a skill branded content studios could sell, it is important to understand what was going on in the advertising industry overall. Storytelling and content marketing (the idea that brands could champion narratives people care about) grew in popularity simultaneously (Boland 2016). They both represented a solution to an increasingly fragmented media landscape where people's attention became the most valuable commodity, both for advertisers and for news publishers. Publishers needed to show that they had a healthy and engaged readership, while advertisers wanted to find novel ways to secure audience attention. This is what led *the Times* to commodify the art of story-telling; stories are a powerful vehicle to get people to care and engage with topics they might not otherwise think about Georgia 2016.

During this time, advertising agencies were promoting their content marketing services. While these two terms, "storytelling" and "content marketing," may seem like interchangeable industry jargon, they actually represent skills that generate varying levels of ad revenue. As defined by Brownstein in AdAge, content marketing "(is) an on-going thematic narrative that helps define a company's reputation and convey its story in concert with other forms of marketing. It includes blogs, newsletters, media coverage, podcasts, social media, SEO, white papers and video" (Brownstein 2016). Brownstein's definition illuminates that content marketing, unlike native advertising, is part of an ongoing marketing strategy that involves various media outlets. True native advertising, on the other hand, is a completely customized product. After T Brand Studio creates a native ad for a client, they essentially lose that revenue stream: *the Times* creates one execution for a brand but is not an active part of the brand's overall strategy. In contrast, an ad agency sells clients on a content marketing campaign that has many components, only one of which is a native ad.

This distinction is meant to illuminate that T Brand could only survive if they started selling a variety of storytelling services. Studios like T Brand are being pressured to turn into ad agencies. Agencies are able to secure revenue from multiple, ongoing, marketing programs. For example, they can go to Lancome and pitch them on an entire marketing campaign that runs ads across social channels, print, and TV. They can sell it into Lancome as an overall content marketing campaign that T Brand may be a part of but certainly does not run. Here, the agency earns multiples of the revenue T Brand generates from just one native ad. Naturally, this has forced T Brand to find new ways to work with clients, to create new products that offer storytelling expertise – despite the fact that the paper was never set up to support an ad agency, one that had to compete with well-established marketing companies that have built long-term relationships with multi-million dollar brands.

The somewhat grim reality did not phase Sebastian Tomich, *the Times'* global head of advertising and marketing solutions. He knew that the T Brand would have to evolve to stabilize revenue, and they would need to do this in ways the sales staff wasn't prepared for. When he started, Jill Abramson was still the executive editor and had gone on record saying native advertising would never occur at *the Times* (Gerth 2017). In a 2016 interview Mr. Tomich had with *Digiday's* editor-in-chief, Brian Morrissey, he commented on how much had changed at the company since 2013. Mr. Morrissey said that *the Times* has always labeled things very clearly, that ads were never called "promoted or powered by" (Morrissey 2016). Mr. Tomich said, "the bar was higher across the board . . . we knew we had to be as overt as possible" (Morrissey 2016). He had seen, and championed, the publisher's evolution in the past, and with little to no support. For Mr. Tomich, going after ad agency business didn't prove to be a task too big. This is precisely the attitude that has allowed him to grow his own career at the company, having been promoted three times since joining the publisher during the fall of 2013. Where previously Mr. Tomich needed to prove *the Times* could create native ads without upsetting the newsroom or readers, now he had the trust of the organization. He had earned the support internally to create native ads; *the Times* was thought of as a company that created honest and effective branded content.

With the mandate for change set at the executive level, *The New York Times* realized that the only way they could generate enough ad revenue to support their newsroom was to go after clients with sizable marketing budgets, brands that are used to working with large ad agencies. This meant that T Brand could no longer approach clients with the mere idea of a native ad execution, but rather the studio would have to approach clients with long-term marketing campaigns. They needed to pitch clients a creative idea that could only be effective if brought to life through multiple advertising executions – much like the US ad agency Ogilvy and Mather's successful "Real Beauty" campaign for Dove, which relied on various forms of advertisements on multiple media channels. Campaigns like "Real Beauty" demonstrated that it is incredibly lucrative, from a revenue standpoint, to sell brands on a creative idea that outlives an advertising medium; in other words, to create campaign that extended beyond a single Paid Post on *the Time's* website.

On a mission to sell ideas akin to what an ad agency would pitch, *the Times* created a new department called agency services. In 2016, a new marketing specialist was appointed to head of the department and wanted to ensure that this new team could operate with anonymity within the paper. This team made it clear to me that *the Times*' sales staff actively hinders the process of selling creative concepts to clients, so she wanted to operate below their radar. The sales team is accustomed to selling ad space and placements on various *New York Times* platforms. However, they are ill-equipped to deal with clients that want marketing ideas. After all, this is not what salespeople were trained to do. As Lucia Moses notes in *Digiday*, "*The Times* has impressed advertisers with the quality of its Paid Posts. But being an agency takes different skills. Marketers expect always-on handholding from an agency, and salespeople aren't inherent project managers" (Moses 2016). Unlike project managers at an ad agency, the sales team expects a commission as well. That is how the paper has always rewarded their work. This is also why *the Times* has had to be incredibly careful about calling themselves an agency. To function as an agency they would need to get rid of sales people and their commission, then hire project managers. This would jeopardize the profitable relationships current sales staff have with their clients.

T Brand has been successful at generating ad revenue, but they have not yet shown that they can replace the revenue earned by the sales staff, despite the gap closing in (Doctor 2015). Today, the paper has come to terms with the fact that their sales-driven organization is no longer the most lucrative part of the paper's business. Rather, the people in T Brand are generating the ideas that are sold to clients. Surprisingly, the people in T Brand do not earn commission on the deals they close. The legacy paper is not ready to reimagine their sales department yet, but early in 2018 they made one novel move: they hired an advertising agency veteran in a newly minted position. Kathleen Diamantakis, who previously worked at Ogilvy & Mather, was appointed managing director of strategy at T Brand. She is the first executive level appointment *the Times* has made who comes from an ad agency, without any publishing experience.

These changes beg the question, what is *The New York Times*' current plan to generate advertising revenue as they make the transition into an ad agency model?

## Samsung: one future model of native advertising

In shifting their emphasis from one-off native campaigns to more sustained, customized advertising opportunities for brands, T Brand Studio has begun to change the rules around how the paper places and promotes native work. These new client relationships – called "partnerships" by the studio – are a departure from *the Times*' earlier promoted content, as their presentation is murkier, devoid of the standard formatting and labeling that characterizes paid posts. Indeed, it can be extremely difficult to know whether an advertiser paid them to produce the content in question. A good example of this murkiness is the 2016 campaign T Brand Studio executed for Samsung. Samsung approached T Brand asking for a "never been done before" marketing opportunity. They did not want a paid post or a native ad in the traditional sense, but instead hoped to create something brand new that was an organic expression of Samsung's technology and capabilities. This request came in during an opportune moment for the paper. In late 2015 *the Times* had made a significant investment in Virtual Reality (VR) technology. They sent Google Cardboard headsets to over one million readers and made a splash in the market because it was the first company to make viewing such immersive video content accessible on a mass scale (Moynihan 2015). This device allowed people to download *the Times'* VR app and experience virtual reality, guided by the paper's journalists. Samsung wanted to promote their technology's ability to capture 360-degree video, which was also supported by the *Times'* VR app. Thus began the negotiation of a deal that may represent what *the Times* is trying to do with all of their clients who have multi-million dollar budgets: sell them custom content that does not look or feel like an ad and therefore does not need to be labeled as one.

After Samsung asked T Brand to come up with an idea, nearly every department on the advertising side of *the Times* worked on coming up with a solution. This happened because it was made clear to the advertising department that Samsung would spend millions of dollars if they gave them a compelling idea. Typically, T Brand campaigns had a budget of $60,000–500,000, with a handful of projects ranging from the one to three million dollar range. Given the scale of the product, T Brand Studio decided to involve the product marketing team, a group of people that observe what the newsroom is working on and find ways to marry the interests of advertisers with that of reporters, trying to find ways to sell ad space alongside content the newsroom is creating.

Characteristically brash, Sebastian Tomich made the mandate clear to the T Brand team: the sky was the limit. It was the perfect time for Mr. Tomich to change the rules for how T Brand should engage with clients. He pushed the sales and creative team to think big, without worrying about how ads need to be labeled, in an effort to generate a steady stream of revenue for T Brand. Tomich was also critical in shaping the pitch to Samsung. He told the technology company that reporters would create a daily video, with Samsung technology, and post it on the homepage of *the Times'* website. The campaign would appear to all readers as "The Daily 360." It would not be marked as an advertisement for Samsung in any way. This was a relatively easy concept for the newsroom to approve since the video content could be on almost any topic, and numerous news desks could create the video. Internally, it was viewed as a lucrative opportunity, not as an advertising deal that required the newsroom to produce additional content.

People who worked on the project were proud to say that they didn't think The Daily 360 fit the description of an advertisement or a newsroom initiative. Therefore, The Daily 360 was not labeled as an advertising partnership between Samsung and the legacy publisher, despite the fact that Samsung spent $14 million with *the Times* on this partnership. That number represents almost half the company's reported net income for 2016 (Gerth 2017). At the time there were no internal discussions about the ethics of working with Samsung on custom native advertising campaigns. Despite the fact that Samsung paid T Brand to produce and manage The Daily 360, the PR and headlines around the campaign never called it a native ad or sponsorship. Instead, the paper's press release included a small footnote reading: "*Times* journalists have been provided with Samsung Gear 360 cameras and equipment to use while reporting out in the field" (The New York Times 2016). A Nieman Lab report mentioned the deal as a partnership with Samsung, with an exchange of technology, and noted that Samsung could publish the videos on their own platforms (Lichterman 2016). Samsung's own press release on the partnership probably came closest to explaining just how much the tech giant was supporting *the Times* (Samsung Newsroom 2017). The release includes a telling quote from Meredith Kopit Levien, executive vice president and chief revenue officer of *the Times*: "It's because of Samsung's support and filming technology that we're able to give global audiences a true sense of what it means when the New York Times is covering the breadth of what's happening in the world" (Samsung Newsroom 2017).

The Samsung campaign paints a picture of the future of advertising at *The New York Times*: when clients have large marketing budgets, and the newsroom doesn't object to working with brands, native advertising without labels will persist at the publisher. All of this also represents a new evolution of T Brand's value proposition, storytelling. Here, Samsung is simply leveraging the newsroom's ability to tell stories, in the form of a 360-degree video. This isn't storytelling in the traditional sense since an ad agency is not crafting a script with a beginning, middle, and end – it is something more powerful entirely: the selling of narratives journalists produce.

## Why video is an easy win for *the Times*

It is particularly easy for publishers not to label native ads in the form of a video. Many people multitask while watching videos and aren't always paying attention to a flash on their screen that lasts less than a few seconds. The disclaimer that the content is an ad often disappears quickly and, most importantly, the text does not always make it clear to the viewer if the content was paid for by a brand. In the videos created for Samsung, the screen simply read, "Journalism by The New York Times (next line) Technology by Samsung." In contrast to the FTC's guidelines for print advertising, Samsung's videos had nothing to do with cell phone technology, thus the content doesn't read as an ad and does not have to be labeled as one. This is exactly what makes video an attractive medium for publishers to sell to brands. However, with native ads that take the form of an article, it is often easier to spot brand involvement, since the editorial narrative usually takes a clear stance, might mention the product by name, and clients almost always demand that their logo appears somewhere in the story. When logos and favorable brand information take over a story, it is easy to see that a brand likely paid for such promotion, even if a label was missing. However, when it comes to seeing the flash of a logo during a video and then a story plays on something unrelated, the content doesn't always read as an advertisement.

This is just one reason why video has become a big investment for advertisers and news publishers. It became a priority for *the Times* when they saw just how much engagement they were getting out of the videos they produced. Though some industry observers caution that video is on the verge of oversaturation, the medium is popular since it is relatively short on social platforms and easy to share. Numerous reports suggest it is a powerful medium for advertisers. *Forbes* has reported that 55 percent of online users watch videos every day (Templeman 2017). Furthermore, after watching a video, 64 percent of people report that they are more likely to buy a product online (Templeman 2017).

In 2016, T Brand took further steps to ensure they could produce high quality videos for brands. To recruit the best filmmakers in the industry *the Times* decided to create a native ad for themselves; it was called The Selects. This native ad, which lives on *the Times*' website, asked people who produced videos to submit their best work. After all the submissions were collected the winners of this open call would be selected to work on the branded content videos T Brand was hired to create. The winners of this competition are now featured on The Selects page where they each have a short write up on what makes their work special. Despite this unique recruitment effort, *the Times* still had to find a way to manage the video needs of its newsroom with that of T Brand.

Both the newsroom and T Brand Studio demanded the talent of success-ful video producers. This created an internal tension among employees. A video producer exemplifies this tension: having joined the company in the fall of 2013 with the mandate to deliver sponsored content, this employee rose to the ranks at T Brand producing award-winning work for the studio. One of the benefits they enjoyed working on the advertising side of the pub-lisher is that they constantly received updates on how native ads were being received by people. This meant that this video producer knew when view-ers were dropping off, how to successfully edit video for social platforms like Facebook, and what themes tended to generate the most clicks. Having to report what is working to clients helped them figure out how to create content that people wanted to watch. Therefore, it wasn't much of a surprise when in the fall of 2016 *the Times* announced they would be promoting this video producer to their current position, in charge of producing newsroom shows. *The Times* made it clear that they have no problem leveraging talent from the marketing side of its business to the editorial side if it will help generate content people want to watch.

There are a variety of reasons it is troublesome for a news publisher to set this precedent. Mrs. Smith and other members of the advertising depart-ment who have made the transition into newsroom jobs have spent a good portion of their career negotiating campaigns for brands. They know what advertisers want, and it is second nature for them to think about content that will generate the most clicks and earn the most interest from people. When someone is put in charge of crafting the video strategy for a news-room, these factors should not be top of mind. Part of this video producer's job is to develop entire a series of programs she thinks *the Times'* readers will want to engage with. She knows the content brands have asked her to produce on multiple occasions and therefore she knows what will be easy to sell to advertisers. Here, it is nearly impossible to separate the editorial agenda of the video department and the pressure from T Brand to develop newsroom content they can sell to brands. Journalism should not be guided by the same principles that are used to create effective advertising cam-paigns. Commercials need to captivate people quickly, but reporters should not have the same mandate placed on them to tell a compelling story even if it means excluding facts.

## Where native is going at *The New York Times*

Often, when people discuss the ethical implications of native advertising, and how the newsroom feels about the practice, they seem to forget that reporters know it helps the paper. Journalists are aware that if they can work with advertisers without sacrificing their vision and mission, the extra dollars help secure the newsroom's survival. When Jill Abramson was working at the paper, people thought native ads would tarnish the reputation of *the Times*. Mr. Tomich experienced this first-hand. When he started his job, a reporter told him, "I feel like you're going to open a sluice of sewage onto this site" (Morrissey 2016). Shortly after Mr. Tomich and T Brand proved that they could create native ads like the Netflix campaign for *Orange Is the New Black*, the organization came around to seeing the value of native ads. Furthermore, when the newsroom saw that, at times, these ads could be informative and did not alienate readers they started to promote the work T Brand creates.

When the newsroom and T Brand studio feel comfortable producing work for advertisers, the rise of storytelling takes on a very different meaning. Here, storytelling is no longer limited to a service advertising agencies sell; it is a skill news publishers commodify by leveraging both their newsroom and advertising staff. While The Daily 360 isn't storytelling in the classic sense, the campaign leveraged the ability reporters have to tell stories in order to secure revenue for the legacy publisher. Each video produced for Samsung did present readers with a story, a narrative *the Times* wanted people to know about – it just wasn't overtly branded.

In this case study chapter, my goal was to outline what happened after Mr. Tomich received a real vote of confidence. The organization loosened its reins and allowed itself to leverage the skills of reporters to halt diminishing advertising revenue. The paper allowed T Brand to work on projects like Samsung that blur, if not destroy, the line that used to separate reporters from their coworkers in the advertising department. Furthermore, *the Times* knew that young people, who would come to represent their future subscribers, were accustomed to such content. In a study conducted by researchers at Oxford, the university found that millennials "are more likely to visit websites where native advertising is present, such as *BuzzFeed*, and therefore are more accustomed to reading it" (Soat 2015). Since the paper has not received an overwhelming backlash to its branded content initiatives they have had no pressing reason to stop pushing the boundaries of what is acceptable.

There may not be a backlash to this trend simply because people outside the organization don't know that *the Times* is intentionally blurring the line between the two departments, editorial and advertising. At the moment, no rule or policy exists that require news outlets to disclose that they have received x dollars from y client to produce z advertising placement(s). Divulging what is and is not funded by an advertiser would not slow down the production of such campaigns, partnerships, native ads – whatever the news outlet wants to call it. Publishers should reveal the terms of their deals with advertisers in quarterly reports and on their website. This is the mandate we should require all news outlets to adhere to. It will secure the separation of church and state, editorial and advertising. It will provide people with the level of transparency journalists should always offer their readers.

Publishers across the country are in the midst of restructuring their advertising departments. They are experimenting by creating new teams, ad products, and sales pitches. Native advertising is hardly a novel concept, but for news outlets, figuring out how to create branded content that doesn't deter readers and makes brands happy is uncharted territory. By outlining how *the Times* has navigated creating and selling native ads, this chapter should have illuminated the issues publishers have when they try to alter their internal culture to keep up with the demands of clients. To generate substantial advertising revenue, news outlets are becoming increasingly willing to work with clients who want non-traditional advertisements that are not labeled as branded content. Publishers know they have to evolve and that change is inevitable, but when their singular aim is to please advertisers and increase revenue, they are harming journalism as an institution. They are deceiving the very readers they are supposed to inform. This is a problem the entire industry needs to address, or at the very least acknowledge. Until there is a mandate that requires news outlets to disclose all branded content to readers, *The New York Times* and other publishers will continue to experiment with how transparent their native advertising needs to be. Without knowing how such transactions are formed, pitched, and sold, it is extremely difficult to imagine a world where native ads don't blend into editorial initiatives. This is the overarching concern when discussing the ethics of native advertising today: people and policymakers need to pressure news outlets to be more transparent. Otherwise, publishers will continue to let clients dictate the terms of content creation, even when the newsroom is involved.

## Bibliography

Barthel, M. 2017. "Newspapers Fact Sheet." *Pew Research Center's Journalism Project*, June 1, 2017. www.journalism.org/fact-sheet/newspapers/.

Boland, M. 2016. "Native Ads Will Drive 74% of All Ad Revenue by 2021." *Business Insider*, June 14, 2016. www.businessinsider.com/the-native-ad-report-forecasts-2016-5.

Brownstein, M. 2016. "Five Ways Agencies Can Figure Out Their Role in Content Marketing." *AdAge*, September 23, 2016. http://adage.com/article/agency-viewpoint/reasons-agencies-figure-content-marketing/305985/.

Chaffey, D. 2017. "Average Display Advertising Clickthrough Rates." *Smart Insights*, January 31, 2017. www.smartinsights.com/internet-advertising/internet-advertising-analytics/display-advertising-clickthrough-rates/.

Doctor, K. 2015. "What Are They Thinking? Times Aims to Double Its Branded Content Business." *PoliticoMedia*, June 24, 2015. www.politico.com/media/story/2015/06/what-are-they-thinking-times-aims-to-double-its-branded-content-business-003898.

Gerth, J. 2017. "In the Digital Age, *The New York Times* Treads an Increasingly Slippery Path between News and Advertising." *Columbia Journalism Review*, June 28, 2017. www.cjr.org/special_report/digital-age-the-new-york-times-slippery-path-news-advertising.php.

Kafka, P. and Molla, R. 2017. "How the New York Times Saved Itself." *Recode*, May 4, 2017. www.recode.net/2017/5/4/15550052/new-york-times-subscription-advertising-revenue-chart.

Lichterman, J. 2016. "The New York Times Is Launching a Daily 360-Degree Video Series." *NiemanLab*, November 1, 2016. www.niemanlab.org/2016/11/the-new-york-times-is-launching-a-daily-360-degree-video-series/.

Morrissey, B. 2016. "The NY Times' Sebastian Tomich: T Brand Can Compete as an Agency." *Digiday*, September 6, 2016. https://digiday.com/podcast/digiday-podcast-ny-times-sebastian-tomich-t-brand-can-compete-agency/.

Moses, L. 2016. "Beyond Native: How the NY Times Plans to Turn T Brand Studio into a Full-Fledged Agency." *Digiday*, July 20, 2016. https://digiday.com/media/beyond-native-ny-times-plans-turn-t-brand-studio-full-fledged-agency/.

Moynihan, T. 2015. "The NYT Is about to Launch VR's Big Mainstream Moment." *Wired*, October 21, 2015. www.wired.com/2015/10/the-nyts-new-project-will-be-vrs-first-mainstream-moment/.

The New York Times. 2016. "Introducing The Daily 360 from The New York Times." *New York Times*, November 1, 2016. www.nytimes.com/2016/11/01/nytnow/the-daily-360-videos.html?_r=0.

The New York Times. 2014. "New York Times Innovation Report." *New York Times*, March 24, 2014.

Nieman Newswire. 2015. "Ads With Impact: What Messaging Themes Speak Loudest To Consumers?" What People Watch, Listen To and Buy, 19 Oct. 2015, www.nielsen.com/us/en/insights/news/2015/ads-with-impact-what-messaging-themes-speak-loudest-to-consumers.html

Pulizzi, J. 2012. "The Rise of Storytelling as the New Marketing." *Publishing Research Quarterly* 28, no. 2: 116–123.

Samsung Newsroom. 2017. "The New York Times to Produce and Publish 360° Video, Made Possible with Technology from Samsung." *Samsung Newsroom*, November 1, 2017. https://news.samsung.com/us/the-new-york-times-nyt-produce-publish-360-video-made-possible-technology-from-samsung/.

Sirrah, A. 2016. Interview with T Brand marketing executive.

Soat, M. 2015. "Millennials Less Wary of Native Advertising Than Older Readers, Study Finds." *American Marketing Association*, July 14, 2015. www.ama.org/publications/eNewsletters/Marketing-News-Weekly/Pages/millennials-native-advertising.aspx.

T Brand Studio. 2017. "Stories That Influence the Influential." *T Brand Studio*, 2017. www.tbrandstudio.com/.

Templeman, M. 2017. "17 Stats and Facts Every Marketer Should Know about Video Marketing." *Forbes*, September 6, 2017. www.forbes.com/sites/miketempleman/2017/09/06/17-stats-about-video-marketing/2/#296cd0601e11.

University of Georgia. 2016. "Consumers Are More Accepting of Native Advertisements, Research Finds." *ScienceDaily*, November 14, 2016. www.sciencedaily.com/releases/2016/11/161114093511.htm.

# 5  The future

## The end of (native) advertising and the afterlife of news

As this book goes to press, assertions of the bright future of native advertising are easy to come by. Newsletters from the US-based Overlap League and the Copenhagen-based Native Advertising Institute describe the emergence of new content studios and the increased professionalization of the industry. A December 2017 survey conducted by the Native Advertising Institute in tandem with the International News Media Association showed global growth in native advertising in news, with revenue increasing from 11 percent in 2016 to 18 percent in 2017 (Eliasson 2017). And industry analysts looking at the year ahead predict that two major developments in the advertising ecosystem would further galvanize the content industry: first, the 2018 EU General Data Protection Regulation, which may eventually limit the amount of tracking advertisers can perform, and second, forthcoming changes to the Chrome and Safari browsers that may automatically block some certain kinds of display and pop-up advertising (ExchangeWire 2017).

At the same time, however, observers have begun to identify fault lines in the digital media space (in the United States, at least) that cast doubt on the power of native advertising to sustain journalism. In mid-November, *BuzzFeed* and *Vice* announced they had missed revenue targets, *BuzzFeed* by a significant 20 percent (Sharma and Alpert 2017). Soon after, *BuzzFeed* announced that it would lay off around 100 staff, many of those in the business division, as it shifted away from its native-only model to embrace banner and programmatic advertising (Slefo 2017). *Vox* has also announced they were moving away from native-only and working with programmatic ads. *Mashable*, losing millions of dollars a month, just sold itself for a quarter of its 2016 valuation and laid off 50 staffers (Tani 2017). *The Atlantic* magazine, whose native program is seen as a model for the industry, has announced that they are rebuilding their paywall (Guaglione 2017). At the beginning of 2018, then, the message seems to be clear: native advertising may not be going away, but it isn't providing news organizations with the revenue they need in the face of the ever-growing market share of the duopoly.

Given these developments, it seems prudent to be cautious about the ability of native advertising to serve as a stable revenue source. The recent history of the news industry is marked by moments of misplaced hopefulness and the creation of failed partnerships or ventures intended to "save" news media: why should native advertising be any different? As I noted in Chapter 1, native advertising's proponents in the news industry argue that native advertising studios are the industry's best hope to take back the control over advertising that they have ceded to the rest of the information ecosystem. But what are the tradeoffs in regaining that control? And what if regaining control is simply not possible? In what follows, I sketch out some possible consequences for the future of the relationship between news media and native journalism.

## Future one: native advertising is everywhere

At the end of Chapter 2, I asked what might happen if the news industry's investment in content studios met or even exceeded the aspirations of its supporters, and native advertising became the dominant form of advertising content in our news feed. In the most optimistic version of this world, such advertising would be better labeled, consistently engaging, and appropriately targeted. But even in a well-regulated future in which best practices consistently prevail, saturation with native advertising might have some unintended consequences. Indeed, if news audiences eventually consider native advertising (even with labels) to have the same credibility and prestige as editorial content, we should expect reporters and newsrooms to realign accordingly, fundamentally changing how news is reported and published.

The first shift will be in how both freelance and staff journalists think about the tradeoffs between producing advertising and editorial content. Once native advertising loses its "second-class" status among writers, freelancers who now eschew content creation for the less lucrative but still more prestigious world of editorial freelancing may find it difficult to justify continuing to work on low-paying editorial stories. Moreover, given the volatility at most news outlets, reporters might increasingly see the shift over to the content division as a move towards career stability. As more news workers see content studios as an attractive career choice, the professionalization of the field will accelerate, and content studios will increasingly make public claims of their importance to the industry (Edmonds 2017).

For those of us who closely observed the online transition in newsrooms, this story has a familiar trajectory. As newspapers moved online in the

1990s and 2000s, journalists tasked with the newspaper web site were often ghettoized in a separate space from the newsroom proper (sometimes, as in the case of the *New York Times*, placed in a separate building). Their work was also seen by those in the newsroom as ancillary to the work of "real" journalists at the paper; indeed, they often met with hostility from colleagues who saw the news site as a threat to core journalistic values. Over time, however, digital journalists were physically relocated to the newsroom and given the same professional status as "regular" journalists, who were subsequently tasked with acquiring digital skills themselves (Paterson and Domingo 2008; Lynch 2014).

As I discussed in Chapters 1 and 2, content studios at news outlets are largely kept separate from the editorial teams of today's newsrooms, much like the "online journalists" of yesteryear, even though many of these writers once worked in the very newsrooms they now support by writing ad copy. Given that content studios are generally in constant communication with their newsrooms – and given their common training and professional socialization on both sides of the fence – it seems inevitable that the Chinese Wall between the two divisions will eventually be seen more as a Berlin Wall, a relic of a former regime that forced an arbitrary division for purely ideological purposes. There is anecdotal evidence that native advertising is being increasingly recognized as part of the journalistic continuum: in early 2018, for example, an Australian awards competition for technology journalism added a category for "corporate reporting," in order to recognize technology journalism written as part of a native campaign while also recognizing the fact that many Australian tech journalists "livelihood now involves writing corporate content" (Sims 2018).

Will this ultimately mean that most journalists' workflow could include both editorial and advertising content? In this scenario, I think that would be inevitable. Already, a 2017 Native Advertising Institute/IMNA study shows that nearly half of all news editors are willing to use editorial staff to produce native content (Laursen 2017), and broader acceptance of the practice seems a natural consequence of increased comfort with native advertising. Indeed, as newsroom budgets are drained, it is conceivable that in some markets that some kinds of stories – stories that are expensive and difficult to report, or the thankless, tedious stories that constitute civic journalism – might only be written with the help of corporate or organizational sponsors and partners. Chapter 3 described several cases where this kind of story sponsorship has already occurred, and there is every reason to imagine that the practice will become more prevalent. Beyond this, freelancers interested in ambitious investigative work might increasingly reframe their pitches as potential native content in order to get their stories bankrolled.

In a 2016 article for *The Baffler*, writer Jacob Silverman painted a dystopian vision in which the rise of native advertising not only seduces journalists away from writing editorial content, but also deters some potential
interview subjects from speaking to journalists' sources, as they hold out
for the kinder coverage produced by content studios. Silverman explains:

> Who would bother pitching a story to *The Atlantic* for $100 when you
> could pitch yourself as a copywriter and make twenty times as much?
> And why would a Fortune 500 executive respond to a journalist's
> questions when he could just hire *The Atlantic* to produce a glittering,
> 1,200-word advertorial instead and then buy some promoted tweets to
> ensure it racks up shares?
>
> (Silverman 2016)

Silverman's disdain for native advertising colors his vision of what it might
become, but he does have a point; in a future in which native advertising's gentler version of the world garners equal weight in the news feed, it
is possible that objective journalism will increasingly seem adversarial in
comparison.

## Future two: the bubble bursts

In my first scenario, content studios become part of the routine of everyday newswork. There may still be distinctions between native and editorial
copy, but the same reporters will author both forms of content and editors
will consider the assigning of both to be part of their routines. For some
media critics, this scenario represents a dystopian vision of the future of
news, one in which news outlets cede editorial control to the logic of the
market. But as we have seen over the course of this book, others in the
industry are less fearful of this future, given that other threats to journalism's survival are potentially more onerous than the integration of native
advertising into news practice. Given the fragility of the news ecosystem, it
would be far worse if the native advertising boom turned out to be a bubble,
and the rapid expansion of content studios at news outlets proved to be an
expensive boondoggle.

Indeed, the aggressive growth of native might inadvertently sow the seeds
for its demise. As news outlets rush into creating content studios, they increase
the already intense competition for advertiser dollars. A 2016 *Adweek* article
noted that the number of companies helping brands to produce sponsored content had increased from 15 to 600 between 2013 and 2016 – and for those
companies, the average renewal rate was about 20 percent, with the lion's
share of business going to a few large studios (Willens 2016). As news feeds

are saturated with more and more native advertising – some interesting and engaging, some mediocre – advertisers may begin to search for a more novel way to reach audiences.

There is evidence to suggest that this is already happening and that such a search is leading advertisers away, not from native advertising, but from *news outlets*. Though news publishers helped pave the way for the rise of native advertising, they hardly have a monopoly on the form, and increasingly they must compete for clients whose aspirations to go native extend beyond the news space. Both legacy and online-only lifestyle magazines already have a large share of the native advertising market; indeed, the closer ties between advertising and editorial at such publications probably gives these magazines an advantage with certain brands. Music platforms have been working with advertisers to develop playlists for years; in mid-2017, Spotify expanded their efforts, establishing and in-house ad studio and launching a "Spotify for Brands" feature. And though Twitter, Snapchat, Facebook, and Instagram have mainly served as points of distribution for advertising rather than creating advertising in-house, Facebook and Snapchat are in the process of establishing production studios to develop their own editorial content. Conceivably, advertising content could follow closely behind.[1]

Outside of the online space, the competition is about to get fierce as well. The rise of virtual and augmented reality will mean news outlets will need to convince advertisers that conventional distribution platforms are still attracting attention. Only media companies that have the financial resources to keep up with rapid technological innovation will even be able to compete in this space; for example, the *New York Times* has been working with virtual reality to create sponsored content, including an animated VR video for GE in 2016 that won the Mobile Grand Prix at Cannes (Morrison 2016). But as VR and AR evolve, such newsroom-based experiments might seem tame in the face of advertising that might appear on the windshield of a self-driving car – or as part of an AR-enhanced shopping (or even voting) experience. Such experiences will be "native" in ways that are still difficult to predict (Etherington 2017).[2]

Will brands be interested in working with news outlets when they might otherwise work with a digital platform that allows companies to place their own products in a user's home? Or with a company that creates video games with built-in areas – such as billboards – available for product placement (Takahashi 2014)? It is possible that brands, candidates, and causes will find these sorts of persuasive platforms have more sway over audiences than the third-party endorsement of the media.

With these new delivery forms – especially AR and mixed reality – advertising "native" to the form and content of its delivery vehicle might eventually permeate our everyday lives, a layer on top of our current reality that we accept as a price of living in contemporary society. In such a world, the role of the news media in ad creation and distribution becomes far less certain. Indeed, as advertising evolves, it is possible to imagine that advertisers could forgo the news media entirely.

## Future three: native advertising is swallowed by fake news

If we are not yet in Nielsen's post-advertising media landscape, we are nonetheless still in a moment in which the objectivity of journalism is facing perhaps one of its most significant challenges: namely, the proliferation of fictive news articles created either to generate programmatic advertising revenue or as political propaganda. Though fictive news is hardly new, this latest round of misinformation has exploited the technology created by Google and Facebook to format legitimate news content online. The result has been content that, like native advertising itself, is often mistaken for genuine editorial content. In the wake of 2016 US elections and British "Brexit" campaign, the fear of fake news as a contributing influence in both events led to a moral panic, which in turn resulted in government commissions, foundation program-building, and commitments from major digital platforms to monitor content and potentially warn users when it seems inauthentic (Jacobs 2017).

In such a climate, at least some native advertising has been caught up in the crossfire, identified as part of the "'fake news' continuum." In late 2016, for example, CNN President Jeff Zucker claimed that *Vice* and *BuzzFeed* were not legitimate news organizations because of their reliance on native advertising (Gold 2016). And in February 2017, the Fox talk show host Tucker Carlson used native advertising supplements in the Washington Post promoting Russia as evidence that the Post produced "propaganda," discussing the supplement in the context of a larger conversation about fake news (Wemple 2017). In the wake of such claims, the proliferation of fake news has led some in the industry to wonder whether native content had been irrevocably tainted by "fakeness" (Loyd 2017; Overmyer 2017).

It is still early to judge whether the fake news phenomenon will do permanent damage to native advertising, but over the past year the idea of "fake news" has been used to discredit the news industry more broadly in the United States, Europe, and elsewhere (Erlanger 2017). This comes at a moment in which trust in the media is already at historic lows (Nicolaou and Giles 2017) because of a host of other factors, including fragmentation of the media market and a deepening sense of political polarization worldwide. Faced with these challenges to credibility, it is conceivable that some news outlets might feel like native advertising might be too risky a proposition, as it that might further alienate audiences and damage trust (Amazeen and Muddiman 2018). It is also conceivable that news outlets facing a crisis in audience trust might seem a risky proposition for advertisers, who would then balk at the premium charged for native advertising.

## Future four: Facebook swallows everything

As I suggested in Chapter 1, for many media observers, any discussion about media and advertising begins and ends with Facebook and Google: revenue earned from native advertising can, at best, only serve as partial relief for the devastating losses in the news industry that can be traced to the duopoly's capture of the bulk of global advertising revenue. Beyond financial considerations, however, Facebook's role in the native advertising ecosystem has been consistently problematic, adding another layer of uncertainty to the emerging industry. In April of 2016, when Facebook introduced new policies for tagging and identification of native advertising, industry pundits predicted that the platform had "killed" native advertising by causing advertisers to reassess the added value of working with in-house studios at media outlets. By altering its algorithm to downplay posts from publishers and prioritize posts from a user's friends and family, Facebook effectively muted all publishers who used Facebook as a means of content distribution – *Salon*, for example, lost 34 percent of its revenue between 2016 and 2017 (Moses 2017). For publishers who used a "brand studio" page to as an additional means to circulate native advertising, it meant the advertising was less visible as well. More recently, Facebook has been experimenting with placing publisher posts in a completely separate feed, which would further (and dramatically) reduce the ability for new publisher to reach Facebook users (Wagner 2017). It has also blocked publishers from posting native content on Facebook that was not created by an in-house studio (Williams 2018).

Aside from limiting circulation, Facebook has changed how native advertising is displayed, requiring that all native advertising tag the brand in the post. Before these changes, a publisher's content studio could share a piece of native advertising without such tagging, allowing it to slip seamlessly into a user's Facebook feed. In addition to making the native ads more transparent, the tags also allowed advertisers to begin tracking whether their ads are being seen on the news publisher's website or their Facebook page – potentially revealing that that placing native ads on news sites isn't much more effective than placing them directly on Facebook (Lazauskas 2016). Industry surveys suggest that some advertisers have responded by shifting their advertising dollars away from publisher partnerships and towards working directly with Facebook (Mandese 2016).

While some of these changes accomplish multiple goals, all are designed to increase Facebook's market share in the world of digital advertising. As with all things Facebook, publishers with content studios are realizing that they are trapped using a platform that is at best indifferent, at worst antagonistic to their interests. Unless the media ecosystem shifts to offer further distribution platforms, Facebook might well prove to be the Achilles heel of the native industry.

## Future five: content studios pivot to video and stumble

There is still another way in which Facebook has damaged the digital news industry: in this case, however, the damage is at least in part a self-inflicted wound. A change in Facebook's algorithm that prioritizes video content over links to articles led some US digital outlets – including *MTV, Mashable, Vocativ*, and ESPN – to lay off writers in order to shift away from text and focus on video (West 2017). If the trend continues, it will likely also spur the decline of the kind of text-based, narrative-driven native advertising content described in this book. Obviously, news outlets that shift their focus away from text-based reporting will not be able to persuade advertisers that they are uniquely suited to creating text-based campaigns. But even the news outlets that resist the "pivot" are likely to increasingly face an environment in which video advertising is seen as more attractive to advertisers than text campaigns, in large part because advertisers are increasingly convinced video is more visible (Smith 2017).

As I have documented here, there is already a fair amount of successful, video-based native advertising produced by larger content studios, so it is possible that many content studios will simply evolve and refocus their efforts. But like the video pivot in news production, a video pivot in native advertising has its drawbacks. Not only is video expensive to produce and difficult to do well, it effectiveness in as a means of information delivery has been questioned by researchers: a 2016 Pew Research Poll, for example, found that younger news consumers tend to be more video-averse than their older peers, suggesting that their soon could be a backlash against video content, while other studies have shown that video is driven by technology and business models rather than consumer demand (Kalogeropoulos, Cherubini and Newman 2016; Bilton 2016). As well, upcoming changes to both the Chrome and Safari browsers will result in much video advertising on the web being blocked automatically: while the ad-blocking is aimed at more intrusive auto-play videos instead of native video advertising, it may cause advertisers to rethink their overall commitment to video.

**Future six: publishers give up on native by themselves**

If *BuzzFeed*, *Mashable*, and *Vox* have moved away from a "native-only" strategy, they have not (yet) abandoned native advertising entirely. Earlier in 2017, however, the publication platform Medium did just that, after two years of experimentation with the practice. Long in search of a good revenue model, Medium founder Ev Williams (also a founder of Twitter) announced in April of 2015 that Medium was "experimenting fairly extensively with branded content on the site – essentially, having a brand sponsor stories and conversations aligned around a theme or a subject" (Williams 2015). In the course of such "experimenting," Medium partnered with brands including BMW and Samsung and launched "Creative Exchange," a platform allowing Medium writers to create paid branded content. But while initial predictions were that this might be a good fit for Medium's particular format and style, Williams cancelled the program less than two years later, announcing that the company was restructuring, laying off about one-third of its staff and moving away from trying to build revenue through sponsored content. Critics pointed out that Medium's efforts in native advertising were late to the game and somewhat lackluster (Moses 2017). Williams, however argued that there was something wrong with the approach itself:

> To continue on this trajectory puts us at risk – even if we were successful, business-wise – of becoming an extension of a broken system. Upon further reflection, it's clear that the broken system is ad-driven media on the internet. It simply doesn't serve people. In fact, it's not designed to. The vast majority of articles, videos, and other "content" we all consume on a daily basis is paid for – directly or indirectly – by corporations who are funding it in order to advance their goals. And it is measured, amplified, and rewarded based on its ability to do that. Period. As a result, we get . . . well, what we get. And it's getting worse.
> (Williams 2017)

What Williams is rejecting here is not simple native advertising – it is *advertising itself* as a means of providing revenue for content providers. For him, the idea that in the digital era content is "measured, amplified and rewarded" based on its ability to serve commercial interests is fundamentally incommensurable with the notion that online content should the interests of *readers*. Instead of rewarding content for its ability to attract attention, Williams argues, we need to reward content for its ability to "enlighten and inform" (Williams 2017). To do this, he avers, we need to completely rethink how to support online publications.

Williams is certainly not the first online publisher to argue that digital advertising is broken – nor is he the first publisher to realize that native advertising may not be the way to fix a broken system. And the solution that *Medium* is proposing – a subscription model in which contributors get to vote, in part, how to allocate their subscription dollars – has driven many of the platform's prestige publications away because of revenue concerns (Fischer 2017). Still, it is possible that Williams' early departure from native advertising may come to seem prescient for news publishers who look back in a few years' time at their organization's financial, logistical, and emotional investment in producing native advertising. What seems in the immediate moment to be a lifeline might, in hindsight, instead reveal itself to be the extension of a broken system.

## Conclusion: news after native

In an interview in 2017, an executive for Strossle, a native advertising firm that partners with publishers to "battle the Facebook-Google duopoly," argued that publishers had to come to terms with the fact that they were living in a "post-advertising society" (Hansen 2017). By this, he meant a world in which advertising, whether obtained through direct sales or programmatically, could no longer simply make users aware of the existence of products or services; it had to provide a service to the user, and use "storytelling" (a term Ava Sirrah discusses in Chapter 4) to "create an understanding of [the product's] utility." In other words, post-advertising advertising is just native advertising, or (to paraphrase a line from *South Park*) advertising that evolves to look like news content after people grow tired of ads.

Over the course of this book, I have tried to suggest that if the news industry's embrace of native advertising is to be seen as an evolutionary stage in the history of journalism, it is important to consider not only what came before native advertising, but what comes after it. The idea that native advertising will remain after all other forms of advertising seep away – much like the last fish in the tide pool – is incredibly presentist when we take a longer view, and realize that advertisements that tell stories have, as I have discussed at length, not only a long history but a far from certain future.

Indeed, for the news industry, a "post-advertising society" might look much more like the future envisaged by Kleis Nielsen: a media environment in which advertising is not the primary revenue source for news, noting that "the link between advertising and news that has for so long provided so much of the money invested in professional journalism is coming apart" (Nielsen 2016). Nielsen argues that we may be headed for a future in which the news landscape looks much as it did before it was supported mainly by advertising. That would mean business interests, governments and social movements might increasingly fund media organizations to the point where the idea of a market-driven "neutral" news system would itself be seen as an evolutionary phase in the global history of media.

If Nielsen's predictions do come true, what happens to native advertising at news outlets? For me, the most frightening part of Nielsen's vision is that it describes a world in which *brands* might no longer turn to news outlets to lend legitimacy to their products, but in which the new fiscal supporters of journalism – those who market issues, not products – would increasingly expect the media outlets they support to cast them in a positive light. In this post-advertising world, native advertising might disappear because the difference between a publication and its sponsor will disappear as well. In other words, the future of news *could* look much like the BP-authored *Politico* article described in Chapter 3: content that expresses a sponsor's viewpoint which is seamlessly integrated into the editorial news stream but not considered to be "advertising" at all. In the US, a new infusion of corporate-authored content into our "news" would have all the protections of corporate speech and none of the regulation of advertising, though elsewhere, stricter regulation would likely prevail. In the grimmest scenario, we might imagine that existing news publications would gradually become a series of branded content platforms, and that professional journalism as we know it might be as outmoded as the banner ad.

I don't think that this is the future that Nielsen imagines: nor, for that matter, is it the future that I imagine for news. But it is clear that, given the challenges faced by the news industry, whatever future is coming will be – at least in some ways – radically different than the system currently in place. The problems outlined in this book are not primarily the fault of native advertising; nor, as I argue, can they be solved by either building up native advertising or abandoning it altogether. Perhaps the question is not whether native advertising can save journalism or destroy it, but instead whether we can assess journalism's value in a way that clarifies why it is worth saving at all. Policing the blurred lines between editorial and advertising seems to be an important part of that process, and journalists, publishers, regulators – even media audiences – have a role to play in keeping the two distinct.

## Notes

1 Snapchat does not have a content studio, but it already creates branded filters that are arguably ads, for example working with Taco Bell in 2016 to create an AR filter that turned users into tacos.
2 In June of 2017, Google's Area 120 shared a prototype for native advertising for mobile VR; it is based on a cube that the viewer can gaze at to open the ad. Though the ad is "native" in the sense that it occurs within the VR experience,

there is otherwise not much difference between a cube protruding into a viewer's field of vision and a web-page popup, and the approach suggests the difficulty developers are having in placing advertisements in VR content.

## Bibliography

Amazeen, M. A. and Muddiman, A. R. 2018. "Saving Media or Trading on Trust? The Effects of Native Advertising on Audience Perceptions of Legacy and Online News Publishers." *Digital Journalism* 6, no. 2: 176–195.

Bilton, R. 2016. "Younger Adults Prefer to Get Their News in Text, Not Video, According to New Data from Pew Research." *NiemanLab*, October 6, 2016. www.niemanlab.org/2016/10/younger-adults-prefer-to-get-their-news-in-text-not-video-according-to-new-data-from-pew-research/.

Bilton, R. 2014. "Medium Makes Its Move into Native Advertising." *Digiday*, July 29, 2014. https://digiday.com/media/medium-native-advertising/.

Edmonds, R. 2017. "Native Advertising Grows Up Fast, Shedding Its Rogue Image." *Poynter*, November 27, 2017. www.poynter.org/news/native-advertising-grows-fast-shedding-its-rogue-image.

Eliasson, J. 2017. "Native Advertising Is Growing at Record-Breaking Pace All over the World." *Native Advertising Institute*, December 14, 2017. https://nativeadvertising institute.com/blog/research-native-advertising-growing-record-breaking-pace/.

Erlanger, S. 2017. "'Fake News,' Trump's Obsession, Is Now a Cudgel for Strongmen." *New York Times*, December 12, 2017. www.nytimes.com/2017/12/12/world/europe/trump-fake-news-dictators.html.

Etherington, D. 2017. "Content, Meet Context: Native Goes Physical." *The Drum*, September 19, 2017. www.thedrum.com/opinion/2017/09/19/content-meet-context-native-goes-physical.

ExchangeWire Staff. 2017. "Experts Predict: How Native Will Evolve in 2018." *ExchangeWire*, December 19, 2017. www.exchangewire.com/blog/2017/12/19/experts-predict-native-evolve-2018/.

Fischer, S. 2017. "Publishers Flee Medium Amid Business Model Changes." *Axios*, June 14, 2017. www.axios.com/publishers-flee-medium-amid-business-model-changes-1513302941-197883e2-a037-4456-a650–3ae2ec02f28b.html.

Gold, H. 2016. "Jeff Zucker Praises Corey Lewandowski, Slams Vice and BuzzFeed." *Politico*, August 2, 2016. www.politico.com/blogs/on-media/2016/08/jeff-zucker-praises-corey-lewandowski-slams-vice-and-BuzzFeed-226574.

Guaglione, S. 2017. "'The Atlantic' Rebuilds Paywall for 2018." *Mediapost*, December 18, 2017. www.mediapost.com/publications/article/311778/the-atlantic-rebuilds-paywall-for-2018.html.

Hansen, T. B. 2017. "Rickard Lawson: 'We're Now in a Post-Advertising Society'." *Native Advertising Institute*, May 5, 2017. https://nativeadvertisinginstitute.com/blog/post-advertising-society/.

Jacobs, B. 2017. "DC Eyes Tighter Regulations on Facebook and Google as Concern Grows." *The Guardian*, September 17, 2017. www.theguardian.com/technology/2017/sep/17/dc-eyes-tighter-regulations-on-facebook-and-google-as-concern-grows.

Kalogeropoulos, A., Cherubini, F. and Newman, N. 2016. "The Future of Online News Video." *Reuters Institute*. www.digitalnewsreport.org/publications/2016/future-online-news-video/.

Laursen, J. 2017. Native Advertising Trends in News Media. *Native Advertising Institute* and *IMNA*, December, 2017. https://nativeadvertisinginstitute.com/wp-content/uploads/2017/12/inma_2017NativeAdvertising.pdf.

Lazauskas, J. 2016. "Did Facebook Just Deliver a Crushing Blow to Native Advertising?" *Fast Company*, July 22, 2016. www.fastcompany.com/3061204/did-facebook-just-deliver-a-crushing-blow-to-native-advertising.

Loyd, K. 2017. "How 'Fake News' Disrupts Sponsored and Native Advertising." *VI Marketing and Branding*. https://blog.vimarketingandbranding.com/how-fake-news-disrupts-sponsored-and-native-advertising.

Lynch, L. 2014. "A Huge Culture Change: Newsrooms at La Presse and the Montreal Gazette Reflect on the Shift to Digital-First." *ISOJ Journal* 4, no. 1: 43–61.

Mandese, J. 2016. "Native Ad Plans Shift from Publishers to Social, Facebook Dominates By Wide Margin. *MediaPost*, December 5, 2016. https://www.mediapost.com/publications/article/290315/native-ad-plans-shift-from-publishers-to-social-f.html.

Morrison, M. 2016. "NYT VR Work Wins Mobile Grand Prix at Cannes." *Advertising Age*, June 22, 2016. http://adage.com/article/special-report-cannes-lions/york-times-ge-mini-vr-work-wins-mobile-grand-prix/304639/.

Moses, L. 2017. "Facebook Is Getting Ready to Test Paid Subscriptions with Publications." *Digiday*, July 10, 2017. https://digiday.com/media/facebook-ready-roll-paid-subscriptions-publications/.

Nicolaou, A. and Giles, C. 2017. "Public Trust in Media at All Time Low, Research Shows." *Financial Times*, January 15, 2017. www.ft.com/content/fa332f58-d9bf-11e6-944b-e7eb37a6aa8e.

Nielsen, R. K. 2016. "News after Advertising May Look Like News before Advertising." *NiemanLab*, December, 2016. www.niemanlab.org/2016/12/news-after-advertising-may-look-like-news-before-advertising.

Overmyer, K. 2017. "Fake News Might Kill the Future of Native Advertising." *Skyword*, February 1, 2017. www.skyword.com/contentstandard/marketing/fake-news-might-kill-the-future-of-native-advertising/.

Paterson, C. A. and Domingo, D. eds. 2008. *Making Online News: The Ethnography of New Media Production*. Vol. 1. New York, NY: Peter Lang.

Reed, J. 2017. "Medium Lays Off 50, Cancels Native Ad Program: An Enterprisey Take." *Diginomica*, January 9, 2017. http://diginomica.com/2017/01/09/medium-lays-off-50-cancels-native-ad-program-an-enterprisey-take.

Sharma, A. and Lukas, I. A. 2017. "Buzzfeed Set To Miss Revenue Target, Signaling Turbulence In Media." *Wall Street Journal*, November 16, 2017. www.wsj.com/articles/buzzfeed-set-to-miss-revenue-target-signaling-turbulence-in-media-1510861771.

Silverman, J. 2016. "The Rest Is Advertising: Confessions of a Sponsored Content Writer." *The Baffler*, no. 30, March, 2016. http://thebaffler.com/salvos/rest-advertising.

Slefo, G. 2017. "Want a Successful Native Ad Campaign? That'll Be $450,000, Please." *Advertising Age*, February 2, 2017. http://adage.com/article/digital/native-content-yielding-big-returns-publishers/307799.

Smith, G. 2017. "Publishers Are Making More Video: Whether You Want It or Not." *Bloomberg*, August 29, 2017. www.bloomberg.com/news/articles/2017-08-29/publishers-are-making-more-video-whether-you-want-it-or-not.

Takahashi, D. 2014. "MediaSpike Creates Cool in-Game Native Ads for Virtual Reality." *VentureBeat*, December 8, 2014. https://venturebeat.com/2014/12/08/mediaspike-creates-cool-in-game-native-ads-for-virtual-reality.

Tani, M. 2017. "Leaked Mashable Documents Show How Bleak Things Were before Ziff Davis Came to the Rescue." *Business Insider*, October 18, 2017. http://uk.businessinsider.com/mashables-financial-statements-paint-a-bleak-picture-2017-12?r=US&IR=T.

Wagner, K. 2017. "Publishers Might Have to Start Paying Facebook If They Want Anyone to See Their Stories." *Recode*. October 23, 2017. www.recode.net/2017/10/23/16525192/facebook-explore-feed-news-media-audience-reach-traffic-test.

Wemple, E. 2017. "The Stupendously Dishonest Tucker Carlson." *Washington Post*, February 15, 2017. www.washingtonpost.com/blogs/erik-wemple/wp/2017/02/15/the-stupendously-dishonest-tucker-carlson/?utm_term=.0dee8d9f2d6e.

West, J. 2017. "Publishers Are Desperately Pivoting to Video: But They Should Be Standing Up to Facebook." *Quartz*, July 26, 2017. https://qz.com/1038396/publishers-are-desperately-pivoting-to-video-but-they-should-be-standing-up-to-facebook/.

Willens, M. 2016. "Back to Our Sponsor? Why Publishers Struggle to Renew Native Advertising." *Digiday*, August 15, 2016. https://digiday.com/media/back-sponsor-publishers-struggling-score-native-ad-renewals/.

Williams, E. 2016. "How Does Branded Content Work On Medium?" *Medium Blog*. Archived at https://getpocket.com/@dttg/share/1122594.

Williams, E. 2017. "Renewing Medium's Focus." *Medium*, January 4, 2017. https://blog.medium.com/renewing-mediums-focus-98f374a960be.

Williams, R. 2018. "Facebook Tightens Rules on Branded Content." *Mobile Marketer*, January 26, 2018. www.mobilemarketer.com/news/facebook-tightens-rules-on-branded-content/515642/.

# Index

Printed in the United States
by Baker & Taylor Publisher Services